Transport Systems

How Your Body Changes and Uses Food, Water, and Air

DEVELOPED IN COOPERATION

WITH

STATEN ISLAND CHILDREN'S MUSEUM

STATEN ISLAND, NEW YORK

Copyright © 1995 by Scholastic Inc.   All rights reserved. Published by Scholastic Inc.   Printed in the U.S.A.
ISBN 0-590-27714-6
1 2 3 4 5 6 7 8 9 10   09   01 00 99 98 97 96 95 94

THE HUMAN BODY IS MADE UP OF COMPLEX SYSTEMS THAT INTERACT TO KEEP AN INDIVIDUAL ALIVE.

Transport Systems

The human body has systems that change materials and move them throughout the body.

The digestive system and the respiratory system supply to the circulatory system certain materials that the body needs.

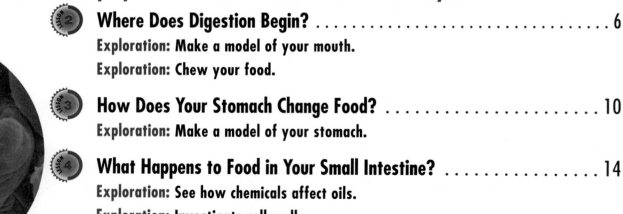

The circulatory system carries materials from the digestive and respiratory systems to and from all the body's cells.

A person makes decisions that affect the health of the body's transport systems.

Think Tank: Design a Transport Game Exploration Lab

Three Systems, One Job

You know that your lungs take in air. You also know that your stomach helps break down the food you eat. And you know that your heart pumps your blood through your body. What you might not realize is that these three jobs are really parts of one bigger job.

Your respiratory system and your digestive system are a little like two factories. One factory makes CD players and the other makes CDs; one isn't much use without the other. Your circulatory system is like the trucks that carry the CDs and the players to the store; without the trucks, nobody gets to enjoy the music.

What do you know about materials that move inside you?

Transport means "to move." The three systems that you're about to study all move materials through your body. Work with your class to make a list of what you already know about these systems.

What do you want to know?

Make a second list with your class. This time, list questions you have about transport. You could start your list with a question about the picture: What do red blood cells have to do with transport?

How will you find out?

You and your partners are going to make models of many of the processes involved in transport. These models and other hands-on explorations will help you answer many of your questions. You'll share what you learn with other teams in your class.

▼ Human red blood cells

Using scientific methods:

Look at the lesson titles in the table of contents on pages 2 and 3. What problem will you solve in each lesson? You'll solve each problem using scientific methods:

• You'll make a *hypothesis* – a prediction – about possible solutions to the problem.

• You'll do a *hands-on exploration* – sometimes more than one – that will test your hypothesis. Many of your explorations will involve making and using models.

• You'll *record data* you collect in each exploration.

• You'll *draw conclusions* based on your data.

• You'll *compare* your conclusions to those of other people in your class and those of other scientists.

• You'll *apply* your conclusions to your own life and to new situations.

The Video Mystery will help you get started.

Where Does Digestion Begin?

Food is the fuel your body needs to grow, move, and think. However, most food can't be used as fuel until the organs that make up your <u>digestive</u> <u>system</u> change it. Some foods melt in your mouth, some require serious chewing—but whatever you eat changes once you put it in your mouth. What exactly are those changes?

Exploration:
Make a model of your mouth.

You need:

Crackers
2 plastic cups
Stirring stick
Water
Goggles
Eyedropper
Iodine

❶ Break several crackers into bite-sized pieces and put them in one of the cups. Stir the pieces with the stirring stick. Record what you observe.

❷ Add water, a little at a time, until it covers the crackers. What happens to the crackers as the amount of water increases?

❸ Stir the crackers and water. What color is the mixture? Is it thick or thin, smooth or lumpy?

❹ Fill the second cup with water. Put on your goggles. Use the dropper to add three drops of iodine. What do you see? Put a drop of iodine on a cracker. What happens?

❺ Add a drop of iodine to the cracker-and-water mixture in the first cup. Stir the mixture, and observe what happens to the crackers and the water.

Interpret your results.

• Iodine turns starch black. How do you know if there is starch in the water? in the crackers?

• How was stirring and adding water to the crackers like what happens in your mouth?

• You can find out if some of the foods you eat contain starch by adding a drop of iodine to them. What happens if you put a drop of iodine on a piece of apple? banana? white potato? uncooked rice? **Try it!**

YOUR TONGUE FROM THE TOP

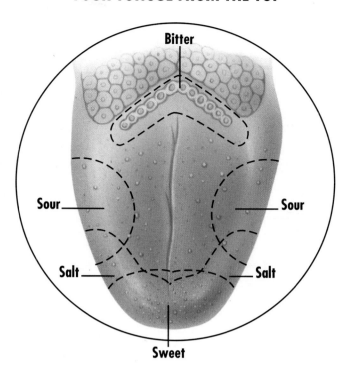

Bitter

Sour — — Sour

Salt — — Salt

Sweet

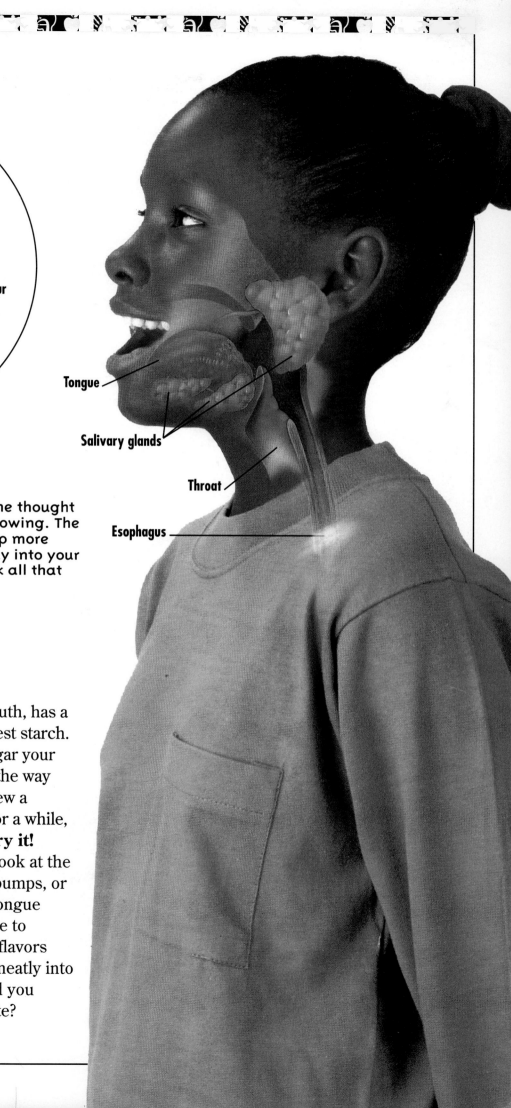

Tongue

Salivary glands

Throat

Esophagus

▶ The smell, sight, or just the thought of food can start saliva flowing. The salivary glands can pump more than a liter of liquid a day into your mouth. What do you think all that liquid does?

Exploration Connection:
Interpreting diagrams

Saliva, the liquid in your mouth, has a chemical that helps you digest starch. The chemical turns starch into a sugar your body can digest. It can also change the way food tastes in your mouth. If you chew a cracker and keep it in your mouth for a while, how does the salty flavor change? **Try it!**

What makes something tasty? Look at the diagram of the tongue. Those tiny bumps, or taste buds, on the surface of your tongue contain nerve cells that are sensitive to chemicals. What are the four basic flavors you can taste? Some foods don't fit neatly into one taste description. So how would you explain all the other flavors you taste?

When you bite into an apple, your saliva is already flowing. Your front teeth—top and bottom—pierce the firm skin and sink in. As your jaws close, your teeth crack off a bite-sized piece. Big changes are on the way.

Exploration:
Chew your food.

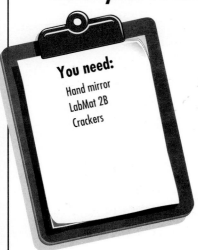

You need:

Hand mirror
LabMat 2B
Crackers

❶ Open your mouth wide and examine your teeth in the hand mirror.

❷ Mark on your LabMat each tooth in your mouth.

❸ Eat a cracker and then examine your teeth again. Can you see which teeth you used for chewing? Mark them on the LabMat.

❹ Chew another cracker while pressing your fingers on your cheeks just below your ears. What do you feel?

Interpret your results.

- Do you have the same number of teeth in your mouth as the number shown on the LabMat?

- What differences can you see between the kinds of teeth in your mouth? Describe the shapes of your front teeth and your back teeth.

- What did you learn about your teeth?

- What part of your body moves when you chew? In what ways does your jaw move?

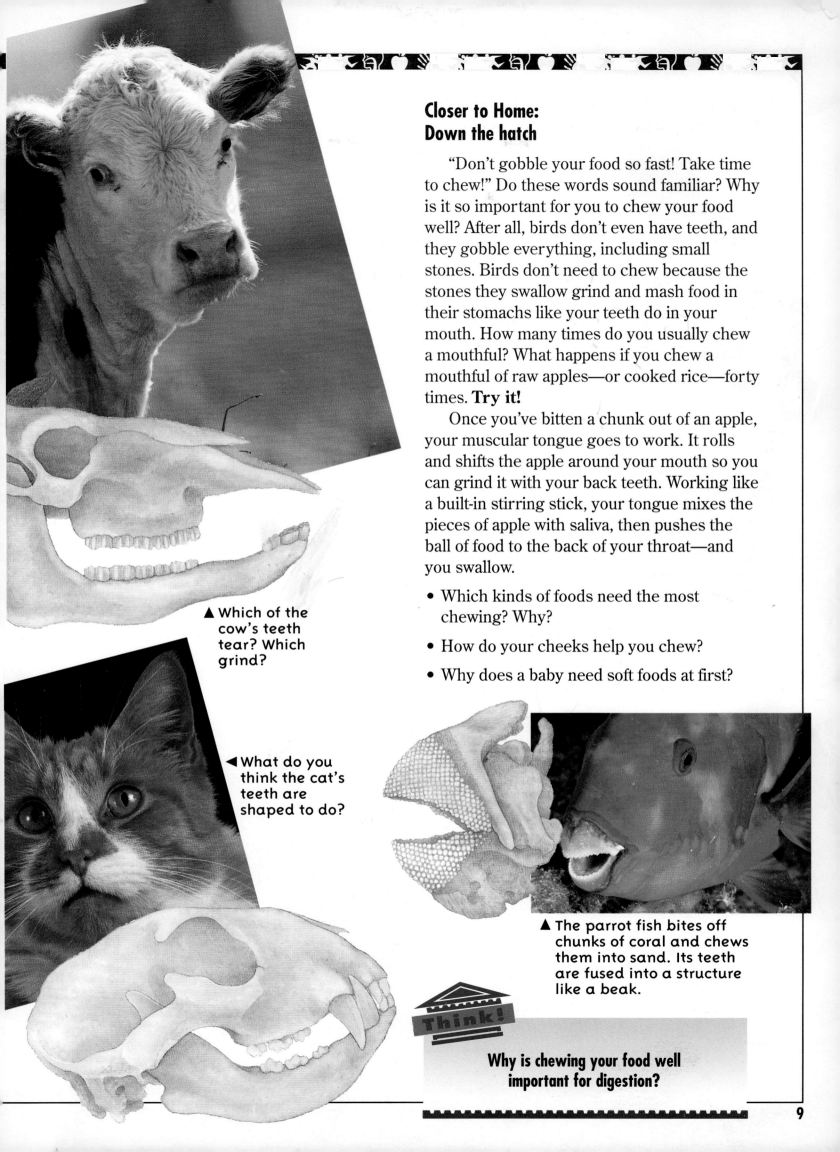

Closer to Home: Down the hatch

"Don't gobble your food so fast! Take time to chew!" Do these words sound familiar? Why is it so important for you to chew your food well? After all, birds don't even have teeth, and they gobble everything, including small stones. Birds don't need to chew because the stones they swallow grind and mash food in their stomachs like your teeth do in your mouth. How many times do you usually chew a mouthful? What happens if you chew a mouthful of raw apples—or cooked rice—forty times. **Try it!**

Once you've bitten a chunk out of an apple, your muscular tongue goes to work. It rolls and shifts the apple around your mouth so you can grind it with your back teeth. Working like a built-in stirring stick, your tongue mixes the pieces of apple with saliva, then pushes the ball of food to the back of your throat—and you swallow.

- Which kinds of foods need the most chewing? Why?

- How do your cheeks help you chew?

- Why does a baby need soft foods at first?

▲ Which of the cow's teeth tear? Which grind?

◄ What do you think the cat's teeth are shaped to do?

▲ The parrot fish bites off chunks of coral and chews them into sand. Its teeth are fused into a structure like a beak.

Think!

Why is chewing your food well important for digestion?

How Does Your Stomach Change Food?

Have you ever swallowed frozen yogurt that was so cold you could feel the chill moving down your throat and through your chest? What you felt was the food moving down your <u>esophagus,</u> a foot-long tube to your stomach. Muscles in your esophagus squeeze and push the food down the tube. A muscle keeps the bottom of the tube closed, until the pressure of the food forces it open. The food drops into your stomach. What happens there?

Exploration:
Make a model of your stomach.

You need:

Paper
Clear balloon
Plastic cup
Water
Crackers

❶ Make a funnel with the sheet of paper and fit it into the neck of the balloon.

❷ Pour 15 cc of water from the cup into the funnel.

❸ Remove the funnel and add a cracker. What do you have to do to make the cracker go into the balloon?

❹ Tie the end of the balloon. (Make sure you don't leave an air bubble in the balloon.) Squeeze the balloon between your fingers. Can you still feel pieces of cracker? What could you do to make the mixture more soupy? Record your observations. ✏

Interpret your results.

- What happened to the cracker inside your model stomach? How is this similar to what happens inside your stomach? Explain.

- What foods do you think would be hard for the juices in your model stomach to break up into pieces small enough to mix with water? What foods would break up easily?

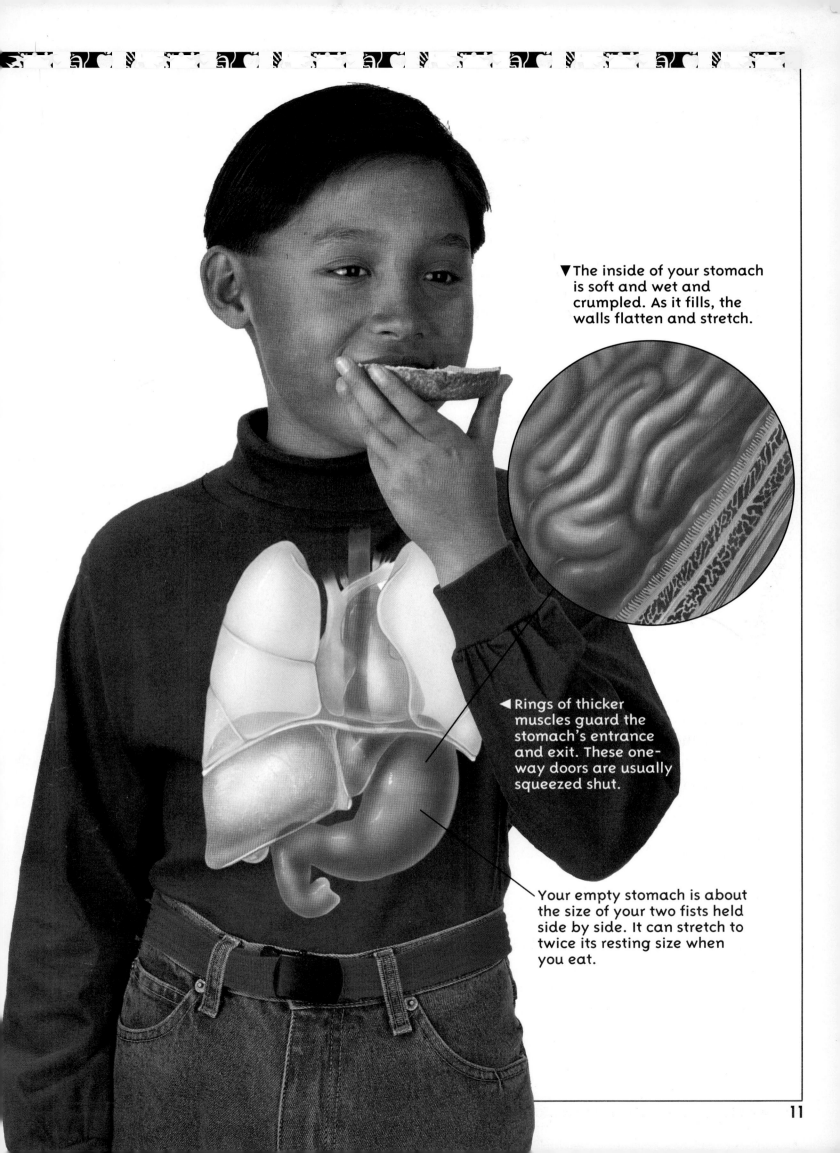

▼The inside of your stomach is soft and wet and crumpled. As it fills, the walls flatten and stretch.

◄Rings of thicker muscles guard the stomach's entrance and exit. These one-way doors are usually squeezed shut.

Your empty stomach is about the size of your two fists held side by side. It can stretch to twice its resting size when you eat.

Exploration Connection: Interpreting tables

The juice in your stomach—<u>gastric juice</u>—is mostly water. The rest is chemicals. One of these chemicals is hydrochloric acid. This acid softens food and kills bacteria that you swallow.

The acid splashing around in your stomach right now doesn't soften you because your stomach also makes a thick <u>mucus</u>, or slime. This mucus protects your tender stomach lining from being digested by the acid in gastric juice.

How powerful is gastric juice? A pH scale is used to measure acid. The scale is shown below. The strongest acids have the lowest numbers on the scale. What is the strongest acid on the scale? Gastric juice has a pH between 1.5 and 2.5. Where would that put gastric juice on the pH scale?

▲ The sour taste of a lemon is caused by acid in the lemon's juice. You can find out whether a food is acidic by tasting it. All acidic foods taste sour. Try it!

THE pH SCALE

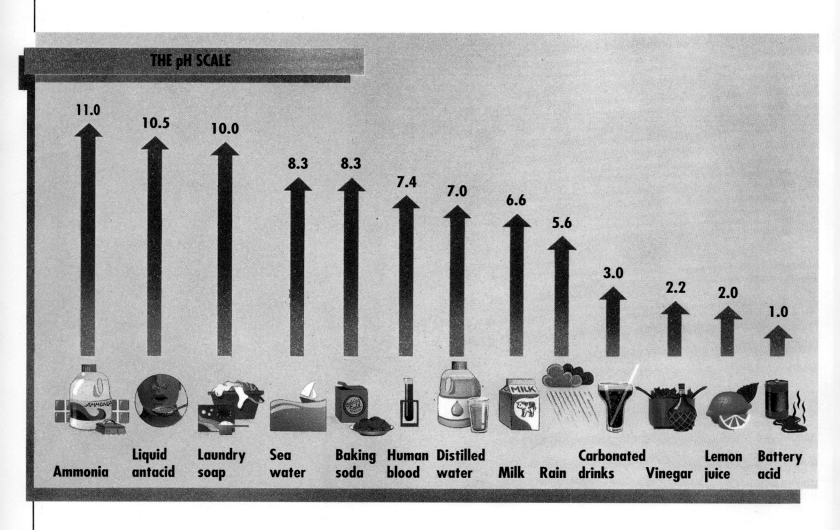

Ammonia	Liquid antacid	Laundry soap	Sea water	Baking soda	Human blood	Distilled water	Milk	Rain	Carbonated drinks	Vinegar	Lemon juice	Battery acid
11.0	10.5	10.0	8.3	8.3	7.4	7.0	6.6	5.6	3.0	2.2	2.0	1.0

Closer to Home:
Hungry anyone?

Have you ever been minding your own business, not even thinking about food, and all of a sudden your stomach spoke for itself? Imagine putting your ear against a friend's stomach and listening. What would you hear?

When you hear those sounds coming from your stomach, do you also feel something in your belly, right below your rib cage? Someone may have told you that what you feel is a hunger pain. When your stomach has been empty for several hours, the stomach muscles begin their squeezing and relaxing movements, or hunger contractions. Even though there's no food in your stomach, there is gas in it. This gas gets squeezed against the stomach walls by the hunger contractions. This squeezed gas makes the sounds you hear and the pains you feel in your stomach when you're hungry.

- Is your stomach always ready for more food? How do you think you would know?

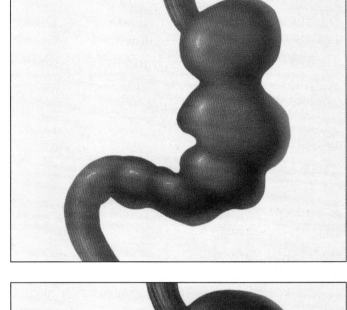

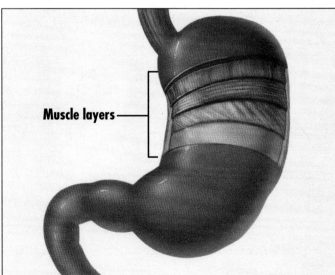

Muscle layers

▲ The outside of your stomach is a stretchy bag of muscles that churns food into mush. Your stomach empties as bands of muscles tighten and relax, and move the mushy food in waves from top to bottom.

HUMAN STOMACH

How are the ways your stomach and your mouth work alike? different?

What Happens to Food in Your Small Intestine?

You do your part to feed your body by eating a good meal. Then your stomach turns the whole meal into a soupy mixture. What do you think happens to food once it leaves your stomach?

Exploration:
See how chemicals can affect oils.

You need:

Water
240 cc graduated cup
Wide-mouthed jar with lid
Vegetable oil
Plastic spoon
Soap

❶ Measure 30 cc of water in the cup and pour it into the jar.

❷ Add 30 cc of oil. What happens?

❸ Cover the jar tightly and shake gently. What happens? Shake it hard. What happens? Now let the jar sit and count slowly to ten. Describe what you see happening in the jar. ✐

❹ Shake the jar again and add one spoonful of soap. Cover and shake the jar hard. Observe what happens to the oil and the color of the mixture. ✐

Interpret your results.

• What happened to the oil and water when you added soap and shook the jar? What do you think the soap did to the oil?

• The soap in your Exploration acted like chemicals in your digestive system. What do you think those chemicals do?

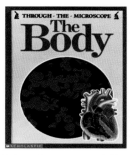

Exploration Connection: Using reference books

Your <u>small</u> <u>intestine</u> is the part of your digestive system where water and dissolved food pass into your bloodstream. The small intestine is not small, just well packed. It's a very long hose—about 4 to 5 meters long (12 to 17 feet) in a 10-year-old's body.

Your small intestine is coiled tight to fit neatly just below your rib cage. How tall are you? How many times would you have to measure your height to mark off the length of your small intestine?

For a closer look at the insides of your intestines, turn to the magnified photo on page 15 of *The Body*.

Esophagus

Your liver makes bile, a fluid that can break down globs of fat.

Stomach

Your gall bladder is a holding tank for extra bile from the liver.

Your pancreas releases a fluid that helps break down starches, proteins, and fats.

Small intestine

Large intestine

No matter what you eat, your body can't use food until it's broken into pieces small enough to dissolve in water. That's the only way your blood can carry digested nutrients, or dissolved food, to all the parts of your body. But how do these tiny particles of food get into your blood?

Exploration:
Investigate cell walls.

You need:

Paper towels
Ruler
Scissors
3 cups
Water
Tape

❶ Measure and cut a piece of paper towel 3 cm wide and 30 cm long. Then measure and cut another piece of paper towel 3 cm wide and 60 cm long. Fold each piece of paper towel into an accordian.

❷ Fill two cups about half full of water. Mark the water level on each cup with a piece of tape.

❸ Put the short folded piece of paper towel in one cup and the long folded piece in the other cup. Make sure both pieces are covered by water.

❹ Wait two minutes and then remove the pieces of paper towel from the cups and place them in the third cup.

❺ Mark the water level on the two cups again. Record your observations. ✎

Interpret your results.

• Which folded piece of paper towel would absorb, or soak up, more dissolved nutrients if it were the lining of your small intestine?

• How does the length of your small intestine help it work?

Closer to Home:
Caution: fat in foods

Do you like movie-theater popcorn? Is it the crunch or is it the butter flavor that you like? A lot of foods contain fats. Some, like butter and nuts, are heavy with fats. Anything fried is cooked in fat.

You need fats; your body uses them to absorb necessary vitamins and as a source of energy. After using the fats it needs, your body stores the rest in fat cells under your skin. Layers of fat cells help keep you warm and act as extra padding between your inner organs and your thin skin. But too many stored fats can cause many problems in the way your body works.

- Read the list of ingredients in your favorite snack foods. How much fat do they contain?

- Potatoes have very little fat. French fries have a lot of fat—how can this be?

- What problems could be caused by eating too little fat? by eating too much fat?

FAT CONTENT OF FOODS

100 Gram Serving	Grams of Fat
Tuna (packed in water)	0.8
Sherbert	1.2
Flavored yogurt	3.4
Chicken and turkey (without skin)	3.4
Milk (whole)	3.5
Cottage cheese	4.2
Eggs	11.5
Ice cream	16.1
Margarine	17.7
Cream cheese	21.2
Hot dog (beef)	30.0
Pork	30.6
Ground beef	32.0
American cheese	32.2
Peanuts	48.7
Peanut butter	50.6
Bacon	52.0
Mayonnaise	79.9
Butter	81.0
Cooking oil	100.0

▲ Which foods eaten in large amounts could cause a person to have fat-related health problems?

◄ The small intestine has a lining covered with millions of tiny villi, shown here magnified many times their actual size. Blood in the villi absorbs nutrients from digested food.

Think!

How does your small intestine continue the job of feeding your body that began in your mouth and stomach?

What Does Your Large Intestine Do?

You've discovered how your body breaks down food into particles small enough to pass through the lining of your small intestine. But some things you eat can't be digested at all. Water and undigested food left in your small intestine move into the last part of your digestive system—your <u>large</u> <u>intestine</u>. What happens there?

Your large intestine has spongy walls that soak up a lot of the water that passes through and return it to your bloodstream. This recycling process keeps you from having to drink water all the time. Minerals and vitamins in the water are also absorbed.

Your large intestine also gets rid of the things your body can't use. Some hard solids—like bits of fruit skins and shells of seeds—can't be dissolved by the juices in your digestive system. If you swallow these solids, they won't change as they travel through your digestive system. Some good foods that you need to eat—like whole grains and vegetables—also contain tough and chewy parts that can't be digested.

Unlike the other parts of food, the parts that can't be digested travel the entire length of the digestive system. Muscles in the walls of your large intestine squeeze and relax—just like the muscles in your esophagus—to push the wastes along, until they reach the bottom part of your large intestine.

Look at the two diagrams showing the main parts of the digestive system. Follow the path food takes from the mouth to the end of the large intestine. Find where the large intestine begins. Why do you think your large intestine is so much shorter than your small intestine? Which part of the journey takes the longest amount of time?

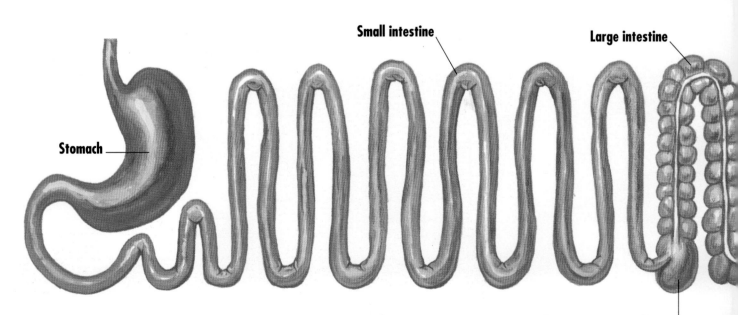

Small intestine

Large intestine

Stomach

Your large intestine is about 1.5 to 2.5 meters (5 to 8 feet) long.

▼ Dinner does not stay in each part of your digestive system the same amount of time.

It takes a few seconds for each bite of food to go through your esophagus to your stomach.

Mouth

The stomach churns and mashes food for one to six hours before squeezing it into your intestine.

It takes between two and nine hours for food to be pushed through your coiled small intestine.

The remains of a dinner might stay in your large intestine for one to three days.

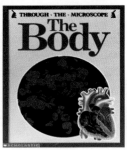

Exploration Connection:
Using reference books

Your body can't work without water. As you discovered in your other Explorations, water is your body's great mixer, dissolver, and mover—it pushes, breaks down, and carries substances throughout your body. Look at the table to see some of the places water goes to help your digestive system make the liquids it uses.

Whenever you eat or drink, you add water to your body. As your meals pass through your digestive system, the water is absorbed and recycled. How much water do you think you take in daily? To find out more, turn to page 15 of *The Body.*

Even if the food you eat is fresh and clean, you still swallow a lot of bacteria that live in food and water. Some of the liquids in your digestive system kill bacteria. Some bacteria survive the hydrochloric acid bath in your stomach and the trip through your small intestine. The large intestine is warm, wet, dark, and full of food your body can't use. There, the bacteria have everything they need to live well and make you feel sick.

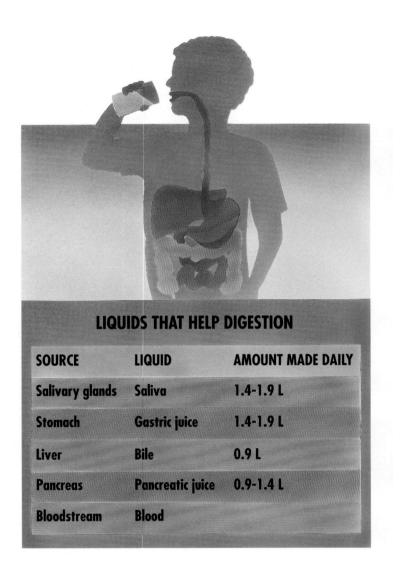

LIQUIDS THAT HELP DIGESTION

SOURCE	LIQUID	AMOUNT MADE DAILY
Salivary glands	Saliva	1.4-1.9 L
Stomach	Gastric juice	1.4-1.9 L
Liver	Bile	0.9 L
Pancreas	Pancreatic juice	0.9-1.4 L
Bloodstream	Blood	

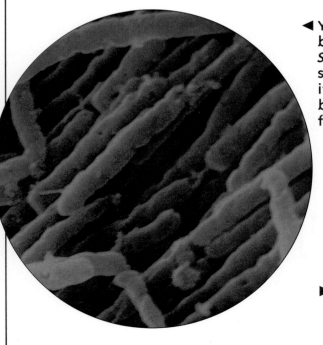

◄ You don't want bacteria like *Salmonella* to stay in your intestines. These bacteria cause food poisoning.

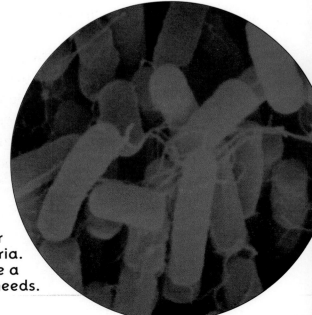

► Your large intestine is a good habitat for helpful *E. Coli* bacteria. These bacteria make a vitamin your body needs.

Closer to Home:
Moving right along

Sometimes the trip that food takes through your large intestine is too fast or too slow, and either too little or too much water is absorbed. What you eat can affect the way your large intestine moves the wastes along. Changes in your daily habits can also change the way food and wastes move through your digestive system.

Your digestive system lets you know when it's having problems. Diarrhea can be caused by bacteria in the food you eat or by eating the wrong combinations of foods. Antidiarrhetics are medicines that mix with the food in your intestines, absorbing extra water and gluing the wastes together. Starchy foods—such as rice, pasta, potatoes, and bread—are good natural antidiarrhetics. So are bananas.

If wastes aren't moving at all, you feel stuffed and bulky. This kind of discomfort is called constipation. You might get constipated if you don't eat enough foods with fiber. Whole grains and many vegetables have bulky fibers that keep food moving through your large intestine. A natural laxative, like prune juice or raisins, can mix with and soften the wastes in your large intestine.

▲ Some foods help wastes move normally through your large intestine.

Think!

How is your large intestine like a garbage recycling plant?

How Does Your Body Take In Air?

You've seen how your body takes in food and digests it to use as fuel. But the food your body digests can't give you energy until it mixes with oxygen, a gas found in air. Air enters your body every time you breathe. You choose when and what to eat, but your body does your breathing for you—all the time. What makes breathing so easy?

Exploration:
Make a model of a lung.

You need:

Scissors
Big balloon
Clear plastic bottle with bottom cut off
Rubber bands
Straw
Small balloon
Modeling clay

❶ Cut the neck off the big balloon. Stretch the balloon over the bottle's large open end and secure it with a rubber band.

❷ Insert the straw into the neck of the small balloon and secure it with a rubber band. Then lower the small balloon into the bottle. Press clay around the straw.

❸ Hold the bottle in one hand. With your other hand, gently pinch and pull down on the stretched balloon and then let go. Watch the small balloon. Record your observations. ✏

❹ Press on the stretched balloon. What happens to the small balloon now? Put a finger over the end of the straw and press on the stretched balloon. What do you feel?

❺ Plug the straw with a small piece of clay. Repeat step 4. What happens?

Interpret your results.

• What makes the air move in and out of the small balloon? How could you make more air move into it?

• Which part of your model is like one of your lungs? Which part is like the area around your lungs?

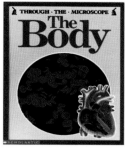

Exploration Connection:
Using reference books

Your respiratory system is like a carefully wrapped package. Look at the pictures below. Your rib bones curl around from your spine to form a protective cage for your lungs. Both lungs are nestled in moist, soft sacks attached to the inside of your rib cage. The <u>diaphragm</u>, a strong sheet of muscle, separates your lungs from the organs below it. Which part of your model represented your diaphragm? Based on your model, explain what your diaphragm does.

Remember what you discovered about air and space in your Exploration? Look at the pictures again and read the captions carefully. Now inhale—breath in—and exhale—breath out. How did the muscles tightening and relaxing in your chest change the amount of air your lungs can hold? Explain.

Your model showed how your diaphragm helps your lungs work. You can feel the muscles between your ribs move when you breathe in and out. To find out more about how your muscles work, turn to page 8 of *The Body*.

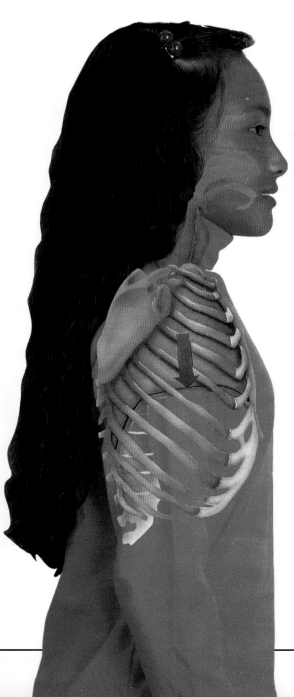

◄ Inhale: As muscles tighten, your lungs stretch, sucking air in.

▶ Exhale: As muscles relax, your lungs get smaller, pushing the air out.

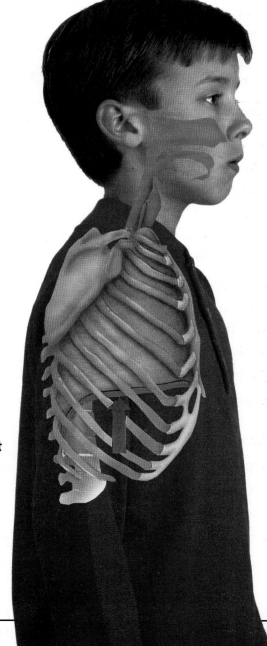

You've seen how your lungs take in air. Do you think they always take in the same amount of air? How much air can your lungs hold?

Exploration:
Measure the air in your lungs.

You need:

Deep, flat-bottomed pan
Water
2-liter bottle with cap
Grease pencil
Rubber tube
Straw

❶ Fill the pan one-third full of water. Fill the bottle with water, and put the top on loosely.

❷ Carefully turn the bottle upside down—don't let the top fall off—and place it in the pan of water. Slip the top off. On the side of the bottle, mark the water level.

❸ Tilt the bottle enough to slip one end of the tube into its mouth. Insert a straw into the other end of the tube.

❹ Inhale and then blow out through the straw. What happens in the bottle? in the pan of water? Mark any change in the water level in the bottle.

❺ Take a deep, deep breath and blow out through the straw. What do you see? Mark any change in the water level. Record your observations.

Interpret your results.

- Where did the air from your lungs go when you blew out through the straw? How could you tell?

- What did you discover about the amount of air your lungs can hold?

- How could you use the setup and a measuring cup to measure the amount of air your lungs hold?

▼ Air flows in and out of your body through your trachea, or windpipe. Find the place on the diagram where the trachea divides so that air can move in and out of both lungs.

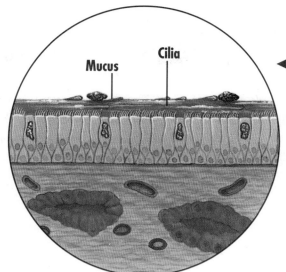

Mucus Cilia

◄ Microscopic hairs called cilia sweep mucus upward to the back of your throat, so you can swallow it, but not inhale it.

Nasal passages

Right lung

Trachea

Bronchial tubes

Left lung

Ribs

Diaphragm

Closer to Home: Clearing your airways

What makes you sneeze? Tiny hairs line your nasal passages, the air passages in your nose. The walls of these passages make mucus, a thick, slimy substance. Dust caught in the mucus tickles the walls, which release more mucus. If the dust tickles too much, the muscles you use for breathing tighten all at once, and you sneeze.

The lining of your lungs' air passages is delicate and sensitive. If dust or other particles get past your nose without being blown out by a sneeze, they get caught in the gooey mucus that lines the passages. Look at the diagram of the lining of your throat. What do you think would happen if the cilia stopped their sweeping movements?

• What are you actually doing when you blow your nose?

• If you feel an urge to sneeze, why shouldn't you try to stifle it?

Think!

Is your respiratory system the only system that lets you breathe? Explain.

What Happens to Air Inside Your Lungs?

Healthy lungs draw in as much air as your body needs. But gases in that air must get from your lungs to the rest of your body. Remember how dissolved nutrients pass from your small intestine into your bloodstream? Oxygen from the air in your lungs must also pass into your bloodstream. How do you think this happens?

Exploration:
Smell the moving air.

You need:

Plastic bags
Paper bags
Sheet of paper
Vanilla
Cotton balls
Plastic self-sealing bag
Tape

❶ Cut small squares from a plastic bag and a paper bag. Place both squares on a sheet of paper.

❷ Put a drop of vanilla on each square. What do you see? Record your observations. ✎

❸ Put a few drops of vanilla on two cotton balls. Seal one cotton ball in a plastic bag. Wash your hands and the outside of the bag.

❹ Line the inside of a paper bag with a plastic bag to prevent leaks. Place the second cotton ball in the paper bag and tape it shut. Don't seal the plastic bag.

❺ Put the bags on opposite sides of the room. Wait 15 minutes. Smell the bags without opening them. Compare the odors. Record your observations. ✎

Interpret your results.

- What did you discover about paper and plastic? Explain.

- Did any liquid soak through the paper bag? How do you think the odor escaped?

- How would you describe the material that your lungs' air sacs are made of?

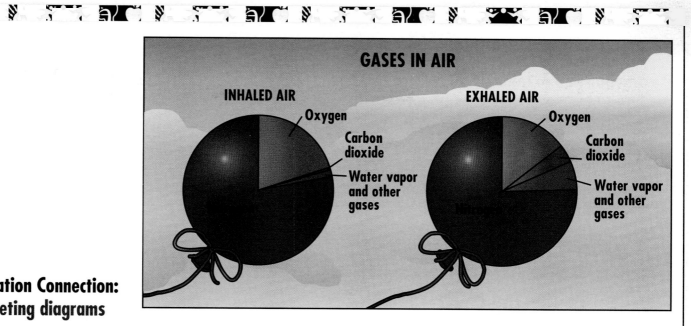

GASES IN AIR

INHALED AIR

Oxygen

Carbon dioxide

Water vapor and other gases

EXHALED AIR

Oxygen

Carbon dioxide

Water vapor and other gases

Exploration Connection: Interpreting diagrams

Take a look at the pie graph. Is there more oxygen in the air you inhale or in the air you exhale? What else is in the air?

The odor of vanilla is a gas in the air. You saw what happened when it was contained by plastic and by paper. How do you think other gases act when they meet barriers of different materials?

Look at the diagram below. Your lungs are made up of millions of tiny air sacs. Those air sacs are surrounded by tiny blood vessels. Every time you inhale, tiny particles of oxygen pass through the walls of the air sacs and the blood vessels, and into your blood. At the same time, carbon dioxide in your blood passes through the air sac walls. That carbon dioxide is now inside the air sacs. What do you think happens when you exhale?

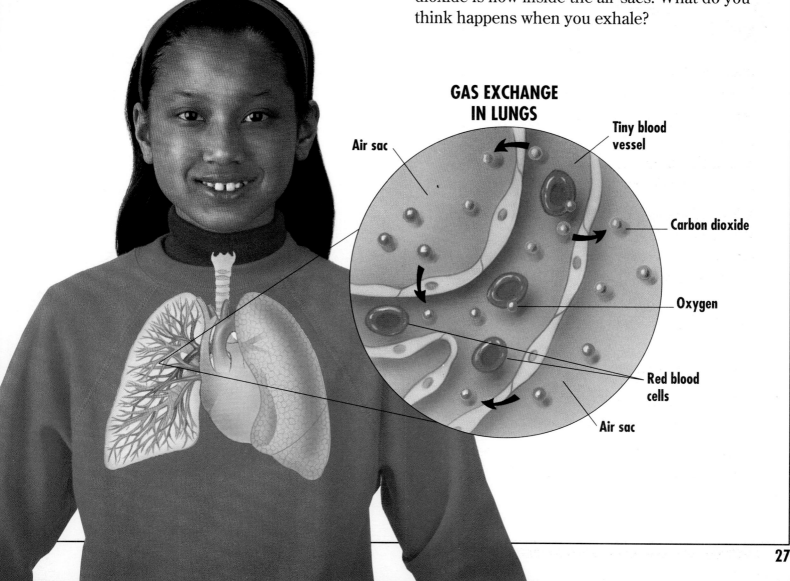

GAS EXCHANGE IN LUNGS

Air sac

Tiny blood vessel

Carbon dioxide

Oxygen

Red blood cells

Air sac

You breathe the air you need to live whether you're thinking about it or not. You know how gases move in and out of your lungs, and in and out of your bloodstream. How can you prove that the air you inhale is different from the air you exhale?

Exploration:
Breathe in and blow out.

You need:

Goggles
2 plastic cups
Marker
Water
Limewater solution
Cardboard
2 straws

❶ Label the two plastic measuring cups "A" and "B." Wearing goggles, pour 90 cc of water into cup A. Now carefully pour 90 cc of limewater solution into cup B.

❷ Using a piece of cardboard, fan air into both cups. (Don't blow on them!) What happens? Record your observations. ✏

❸ Put one straw in cup A and another straw in cup B. Take a deep breath and blow through the straw in cup A for 30 seconds. What happens? Take another deep breath and blow through the straw in cup B for 30 seconds. What happens?

❹ Wait five minutes and then check the two cups. Did the liquids in the cups change? How? Record your observations. ✏

Interpret your results.

* How could you tell that the air you exhaled was different from the air you inhaled?

* Look back at the chart on page 27. The same gases are present in inhaled and exhaled air. What changes?

* When you fanned air at the liquids in the cups, was that air more like air you inhale or air you exhale? Explain.

◄ There's less oxygen in each breath of air you take the higher you climb.

▲ The body can survive only a few minutes without oxygen before brain damage occurs. Bottles of this gas help save many lives.

Closer to Home: Feeling the pressure

You live and breathe in a sea of air. But all air is not the same. The mixture of gases stays the same, but there's less air the farther you go from the surface of Earth. There's more oxygen in each breath of the air you take at the seashore than in each breath you take on a mountaintop.

So how do people who live on high mountains get enough oxygen? Scientists have discovered that people in the Andes Mountains in Peru and in the Himalaya Mountains in Tibet have larger lungs than most people. They also have more red blood cells. Those are the blood cells that carry oxygen all through the body. Larger lungs can take in more air, and more red blood cells can draw more oxygen into the blood.

• Would air in areas of land below sea level have more oxygen or less oxygen than at sea level?

Think!

How do the air sacs in your lungs work like the villi in the walls of your small intestine? What do the air sacs do that the villi don't?

How Does Your Blood Carry Oxygen and Digested Food?

You eat to get nutrients into your bloodstream. You breathe to get oxygen into your bloodstream. What happens to nutrients and oxygen once they get there?

You have about 5 liters (a little more than 5 quarts) of blood moving throughout your body right now. This flow of blood is your bloodstream. Your heart pumps your blood through blood vessels that reach every part of your body and then returns it to your heart. Your blood vessels and heart are called your <u>circulatory</u> <u>system</u> because of the way they constantly move, or circulate, blood through your body. Together, the parts of this system deliver nutrients and oxygen to every cell in your body.

Look at the picture below. A little more than half the blood inside you is a liquid called <u>plasma</u>. Plasma is sticky, straw-colored, and nine-tenths water. Hundreds of chemicals are dissolved in your plasma, including nutrients that entered your bloodstream at your small intestine. Moving along in the plasma are the solid parts of your blood—<u>red blood cells</u>, <u>white blood cells</u>, and <u>platelets</u>.

Red blood cell

Plasma

Platelet

White blood cell

►White blood cells surround and gobble up bacteria and other harmful particles.

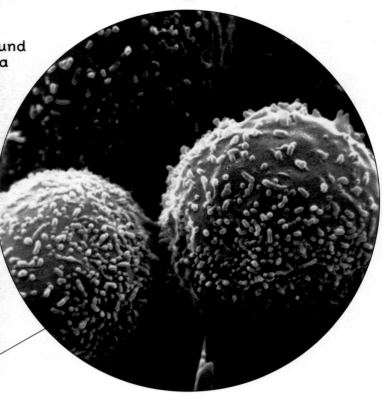

◄ Red blood cells are so small that hundreds could fit on the head of a pin. These tiny button-shaped cells carry oxygen to every cell in your body.

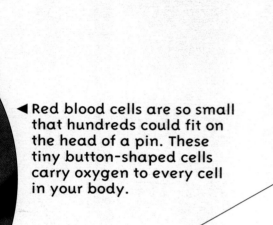

►Platelets stop the flow of blood from any tear made in a blood vessel. If you cut your skin, tiny platelets help form the scab.

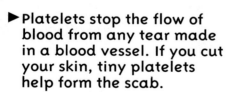

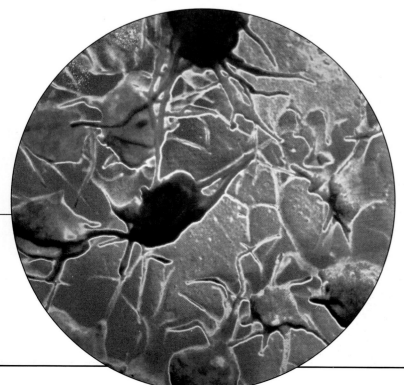

Information Connection: Using reference books

Your blood never stops moving. From your heart, blood flows to your lungs, where carbon dioxide moves out of your blood and into the air in your lungs. At the same time, oxygen moves through the air sac walls and attaches to the red blood cells in tiny blood vessels. Now bright red with oxygen, the blood returns to your heart.

Your heart pumps the oxygen-rich blood to every cell in your body. As the blood flows into and around your brain, liver, and other organs of your body, it loses oxygen to the cells of each organ and picks up carbon dioxide. As oxygen is lost, the bright red color fades. This oxygen-poor blood then returns to the heart to begin the journey again. To find out more about blood, check pages 26–31 in *The Heart and Blood*.

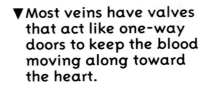

▼ The inner layer of an artery is "leakproof." The outer layer is stretchy. In between is a layer of muscle.

▼ Most veins have valves that act like one-way doors to keep the blood moving along toward the heart.

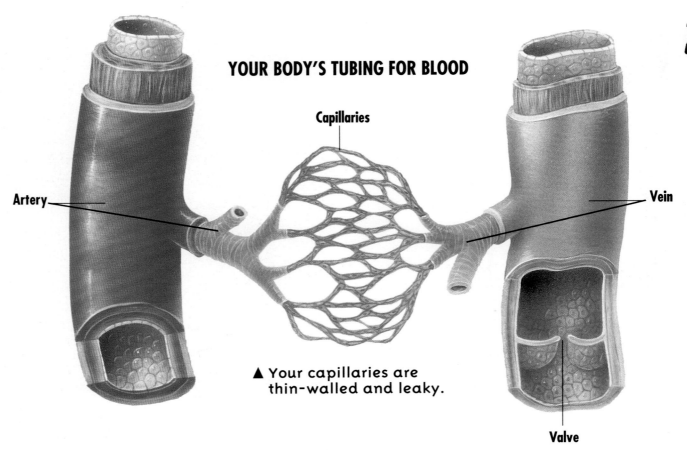

YOUR BODY'S TUBING FOR BLOOD

Capillaries

Artery

Vein

▲ Your capillaries are thin-walled and leaky.

Valve

Closer to Home:
Go with the flow.

Look at the drawings of the three types of blood vessels that carry blood through your body. Most <u>arteries</u> are large, thick-walled blood vessels that carry oxygen-rich blood away from your heart. As an artery moves farther from the heart, it branches into smaller blood vessels, which branch into even smaller vessels, until they can't be seen without a microscope.

These smallest blood vessels are your <u>capillaries</u>. Nutrients and oxygen slip through the walls of capillaries into your cells. Wastes like carbon dioxide slip out of the cells and into the capillaries to be carried away.

At the other end of this network of tiny vessels, <u>veins</u> begin. Most veins carry oxygen-poor blood back to your heart. Veins have the same layers as arteries but thinner walls. The veins join larger and larger veins. Look at the diagram. What keeps the blood in the veins from flowing back into the capillaries?

With a mirror and flashlight, you can examine the pink arteries and blue veins under your tongue. **Try it!**

• Why do you think your blood vessels are visible in some parts of your body and not in others?

Compare the computer view of the circulatory system with the system of veins in this leaf. How are they similar?

▲ This cross section of an artery (left) and a vein (right) is magnified to 260 times actual size.

Think!

Your veins and arteries form a circular path through your body. What does that mean?

LESSON 9

How Does Blood Get to Your Other Systems?

You know what your bloodstream is, what it carries, and where it flows. But how does your heart push your blood through your body? Put your hand on the left side of your chest and feel your heart, a muscle that never seems to rest. How does all that beating move your blood?

Exploration:
Make a model of a heart.

You need:

2 eyedropper devices

Small pipet bulb

Two plastic cups

Water

Red food coloring

Grease pencil

❶ Your teacher will give you a pair of small devices made from eyedropper bulbs and tubes. Push the narrow neck of one eyedropper into the tiny hole in the pipet bulb. Push the wider end of the second eyedropper into the bigger hole. The bulb represents your heart.

❷ Fill two cups half full of water and color the water red. Mark the water levels with your grease pencil. Put the end of one rubber tube in each cup and set them side by side. Label the cup on your right "Veins" and the cup on your left "Arteries."

❸ Squeeze the pipet bulb hard. Once the water is moving, keep up a steady rhythm.

Interpret your results.

• Which way does blood flow in your model?

• How can you make the water move more rapidly or more slowly?

• What does this model show you about the way your heart works?

Exploration Connection: Using reference books

Your model shows how your heart pumps blood. Look at the diagram of the heart. Your heart is about the size of your closed fist. Mostly hollow, it's made of muscular walls. Your heart is divided into two parts by a sheet of muscle called the septum. Find the septum in the diagram of the heart. The blood in the two halves of your heart never mixes. Can you see why?

Even though your heart is full of blood, it can't use the blood it's pumping to feed its own cells. The heart has a series of blood vessels—arteries, capillaries, and veins—wrapped around it to carry the nutrients and oxygen it needs.

Heart valves work like one-way doors between the parts of your heart. The valves snap shut after blood passes through them. For a closer look at heart valves, turn to the diagrams on pages 10–11 of *The Heart and Blood*.

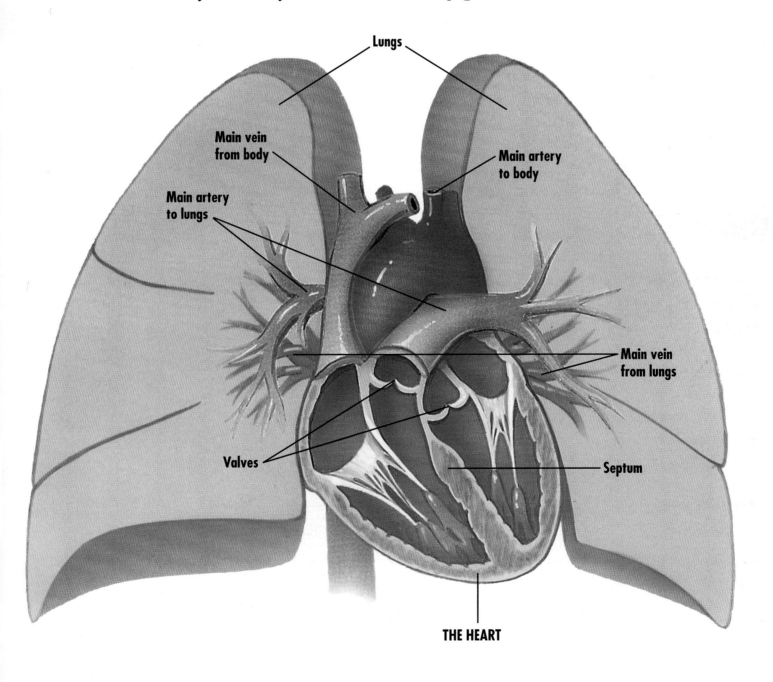

Lungs

Main vein from body

Main artery to lungs

Main artery to body

Main vein from lungs

Valves

Septum

THE HEART

You can feel your heart's rhythm where your arteries are just below the surface of your skin. This steady rhythm or beat is your pulse. What can your pulse tell you about your heart?

Exploration:
Make a pulsimeter.

You need:

Modeling clay
Flat toothpicks
Clock with second hand

❶ Study the diagram. Find the pulse points on your body. Where can you feel your clearest pulse?

❷ Roll a ball of clay about the size of a pea. Flatten the bottom of the ball of clay and push a toothpick into it.

❸ Place the clay on the pulse point on your wrist.

❹ Hold still and watch the toothpick. What do you see? If nothing happens, you may not have found the right place. Move the clay around until you do.

❺ Time your pulse for 15 seconds. Multiply this number by four to get your pulse rate. How many times a minute does your heart beat? Compare your pulse rate to those of your classmates. Compare it to your teacher's pulse rate. Graph your results on your LabMat. ✏

Interpret your results.

• What is happening to your blood vessels to affect the toothpick?

• If you were to run in place and measure your pulse rate again, would it increase or decrease? Why? **Try it!**

• Which of your daily activities make your heart beat faster? slower? Why?

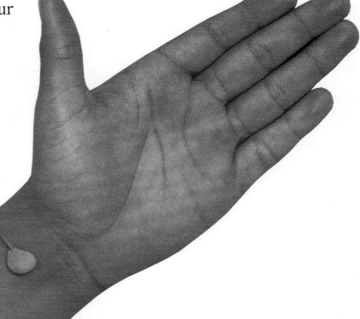

▲ The places you can find arteries right beneath your skin are called pulse points. Each pulse point is marked by a white dot. Touch them and you can feel the blood moving to the rhythm of your heart.

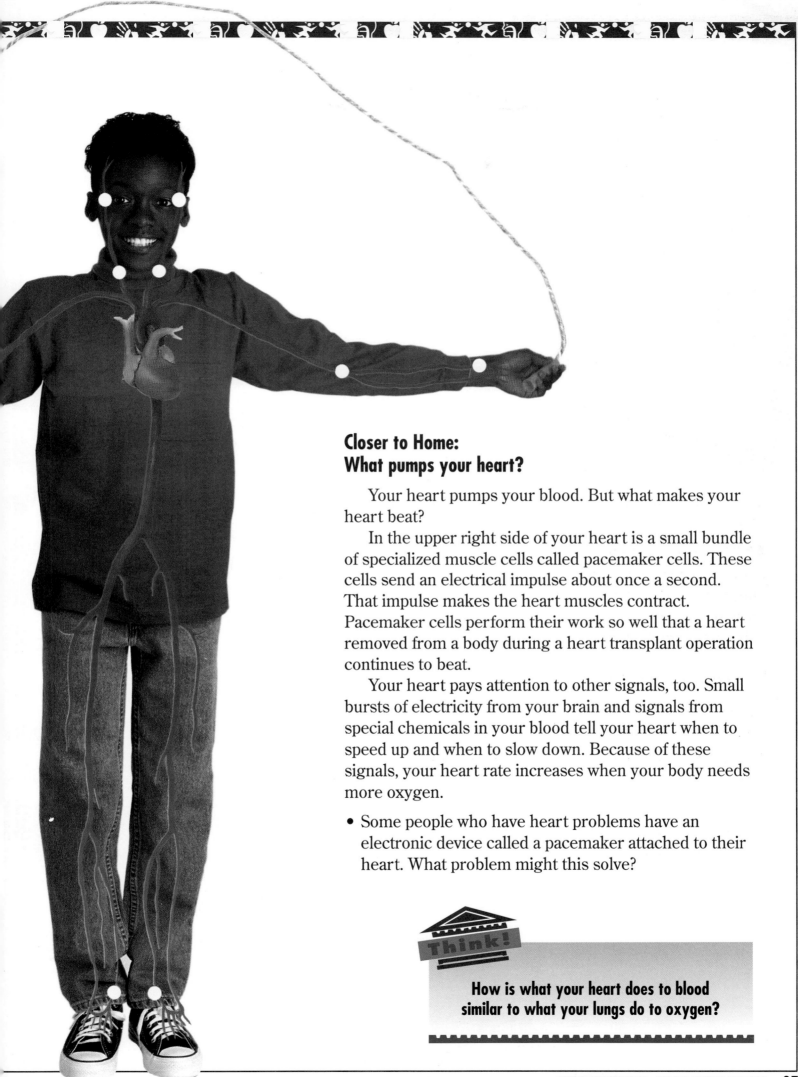

Closer to Home:
What pumps your heart?

Your heart pumps your blood. But what makes your heart beat?

In the upper right side of your heart is a small bundle of specialized muscle cells called pacemaker cells. These cells send an electrical impulse about once a second. That impulse makes the heart muscles contract. Pacemaker cells perform their work so well that a heart removed from a body during a heart transplant operation continues to beat.

Your heart pays attention to other signals, too. Small bursts of electricity from your brain and signals from special chemicals in your blood tell your heart when to speed up and when to slow down. Because of these signals, your heart rate increases when your body needs more oxygen.

• Some people who have heart problems have an electronic device called a pacemaker attached to their heart. What problem might this solve?

Think!

How is what your heart does to blood similar to what your lungs do to oxygen?

How Do Oxygen and Digested Foods Get Into Your Body's Cells?

You know your heart pumps blood to every part of your body without you thinking about it—even while you're sleeping. But how do your think the nutrients and oxygen carried by your bloodstream move from your blood vessels into your body's cells?

Exploration:
Make a model of a cell.

You need:
Herbal tea bag
Clear plastic cup
Water
Clock or watch
Paper towel

❶ Fill the cup about half full of water.

❷ Hold the tea bag by the tag. Slowly lower it into the water. What happens? The tea bag represents a cell. The bag's paper represents the cell walls.

❸ Observe the water for two minutes. Record any changes you notice. ✏

❹ Take the tea bag out of the cup. Squeeze out the extra water, and lay the tea bag on a paper towel. After half an hour, observe the paper towel under the tea bag. Record your observations. ✏

Interpret your results.

- How did water get inside the tea bag?

- What caused the changes in the water and the paper towel?

- How do you think nutrients and oxygen get inside a cell? At what part of your circulatory system do you think this happens?

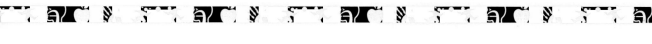

Exploration Connection:
Using reference books

The nutrients in your food and the oxygen in the air you breathe can't do you any good until they reach your cells. You've seen how your body's systems deliver them to your cells. Describe the role each system plays.

After dissolved nutrients and oxygen enter a cell, the cell combines them. How?

The way nutrients and oxygen combine in your cells is similar to the way wood burns in a fire. A wood fire needs oxygen, or it won't burn. The oxygen and wood combine, giving off heat energy and wastes such as smoke and ashes. Nutrients and oxygen in your cells also give off energy and wastes as they combine. To find out what one of those wastes is, turn to page 10 of *The Heart and Blood*.

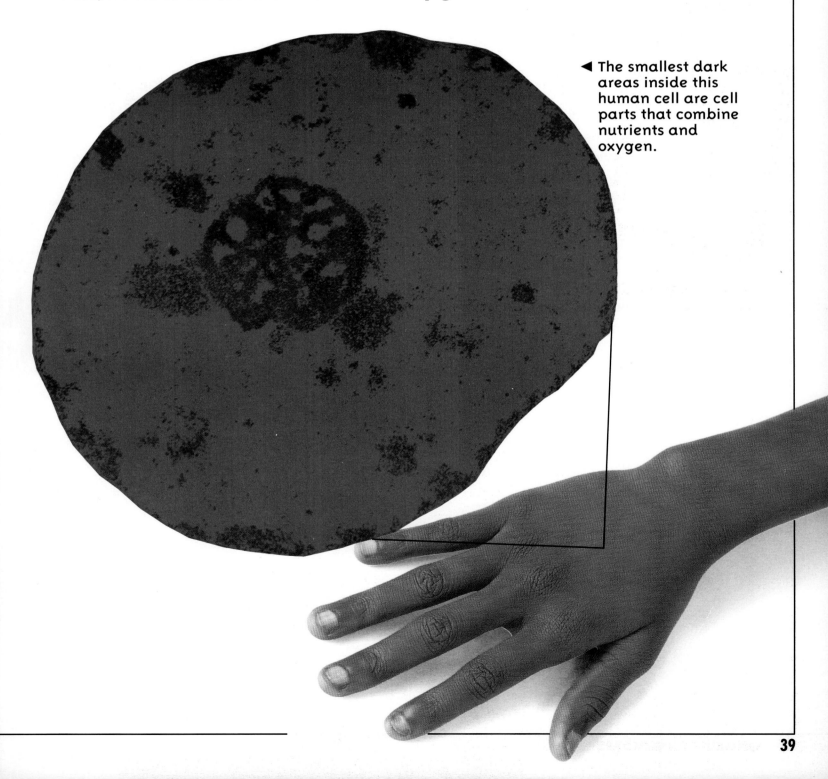

◄ The smallest dark areas inside this human cell are cell parts that combine nutrients and oxygen.

Closer to Home:
Taking your temperature

When nutrients and oxygen combine inside your cells, they give off several kinds of energy. One is heat energy that keeps your body temperature the same, no matter what the temperature of the air around you is.

Heat escapes from the outside of your body faster than it does from the inside. Think of a potato fresh from the oven. Even after the skin is cool, the inside may still be hot. Your body works in much the same way.

On cold days, blood vessels near the surface of your skin squeeze tight so that less blood flows there, and less heat escapes into the air. When you're really cold, you shiver to keep warm. When you shiver, your muscles squeeze and let go in rapid waves of motion. Your muscle cells work harder and combine extra nutrients and oxygen. That causes the cells to produce heat to replace the heat lost to the cold air.

On hot days, your body may feel too warm. When you feel really hot, you sweat. When your sweat evaporates, it carries away heat. You cool off.

A small rise in body temperature can be a good sign. Your body heats up when it's trying to kill harmful bacteria or repair damaged tissue. Sometimes just the part of your body that's hurt heats up. A cut that's healing often feels warm to the touch. But your temperature can only climb so high before the heat itself begins to do harm to your body.

Your body temperature is usually about 37.0° C (98.6° F). You can check your temperature by using a thermometer like the one shown in the picture.

• Do you think exercise changes body temperature? How would you explain that?

• Do you think eating changes body temperature? Explain.

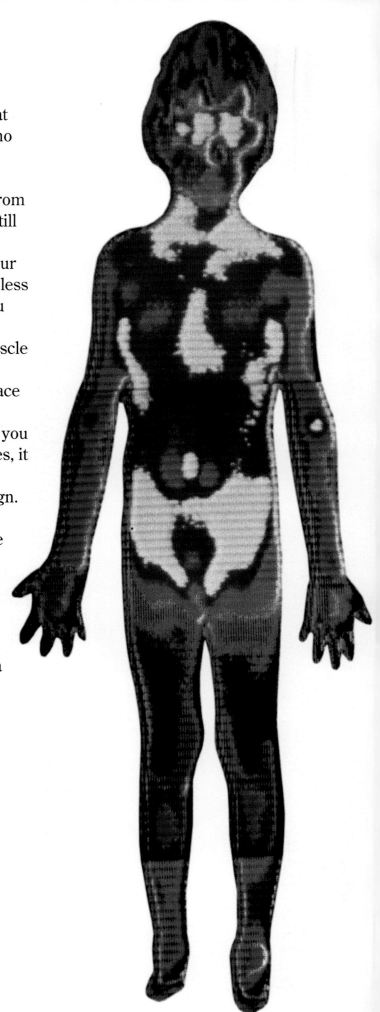

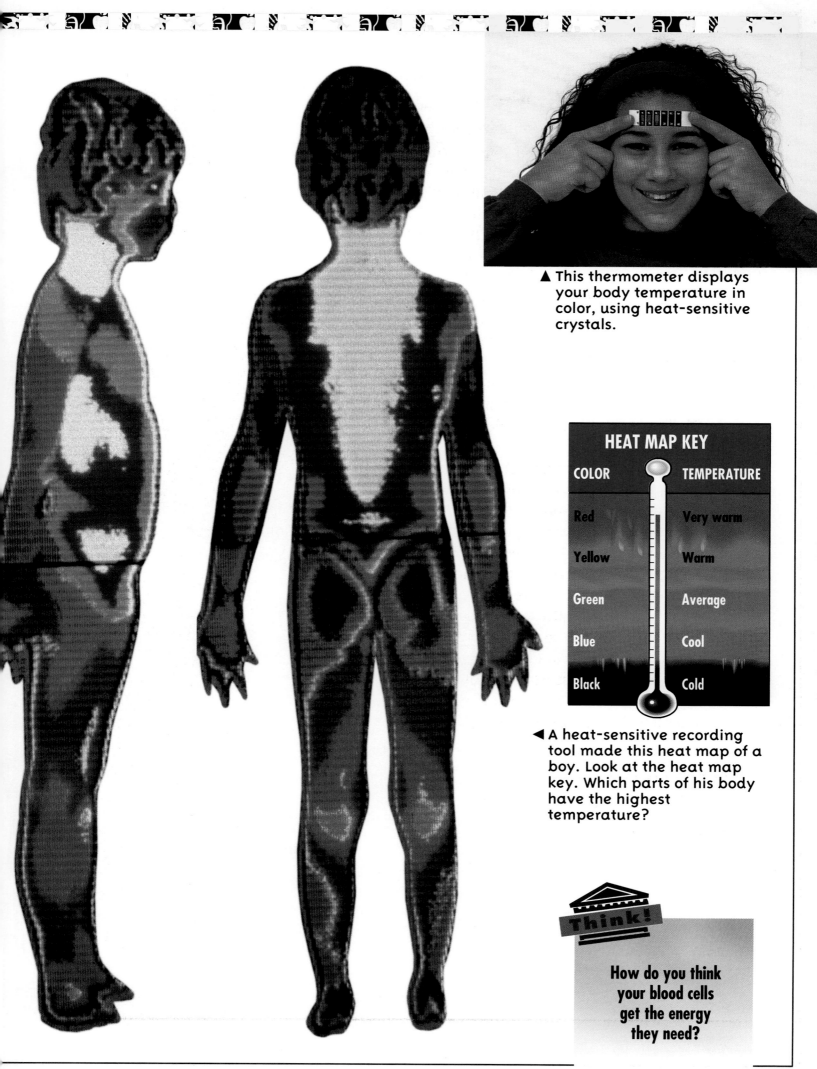

▲ This thermometer displays your body temperature in color, using heat-sensitive crystals.

HEAT MAP KEY

COLOR	TEMPERATURE
Red	Very warm
Yellow	Warm
Green	Average
Blue	Cool
Black	Cold

◄ A heat-sensitive recording tool made this heat map of a boy. Look at the heat map key. Which parts of his body have the highest temperature?

Think!

How do you think your blood cells get the energy they need?

How Does Your Blood Help Clean Your Cells?

Your body is good at getting what it needs. It's just as good at getting rid of what it can't use. Your blood carries wastes away from your cells. How do you think your blood gets rid of cell wastes?

Exploration:
Track the paths of cell wastes.

❶ Find your digestive system in the diagram. Read the table. What moves into your blood from your digestive system? Record your findings. ✐

❷ Which parts of your respiratory system are shown on the diagram? Look at the table. What moves from your blood into your respiratory system? What moves in the other direction? Record your findings. ✐

❸ Locate your kidneys on the diagram. Where do the wastes removed by the kidneys come from? How are they moved to your kidneys? Record your findings. ✐

Interpret your results.

• What parts of your body move wastes?

• What do you think might happen if your body couldn't get rid of wastes?

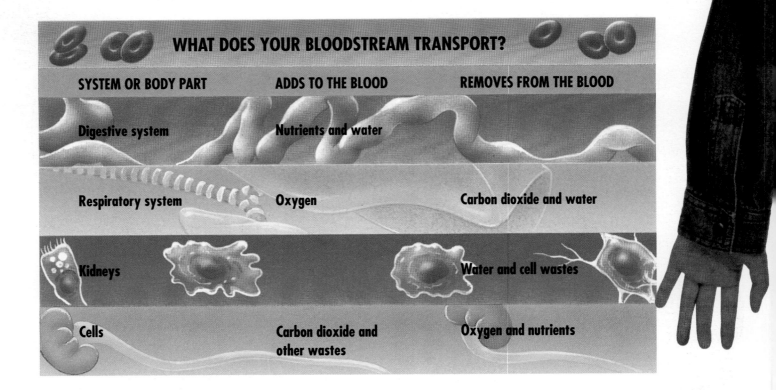

WHAT DOES YOUR BLOODSTREAM TRANSPORT?		
SYSTEM OR BODY PART	ADDS TO THE BLOOD	REMOVES FROM THE BLOOD
Digestive system	Nutrients and water	
Respiratory system	Oxygen	Carbon dioxide and water
Kidneys		Water and cell wastes
Cells	Carbon dioxide and other wastes	Oxygen and nutrients

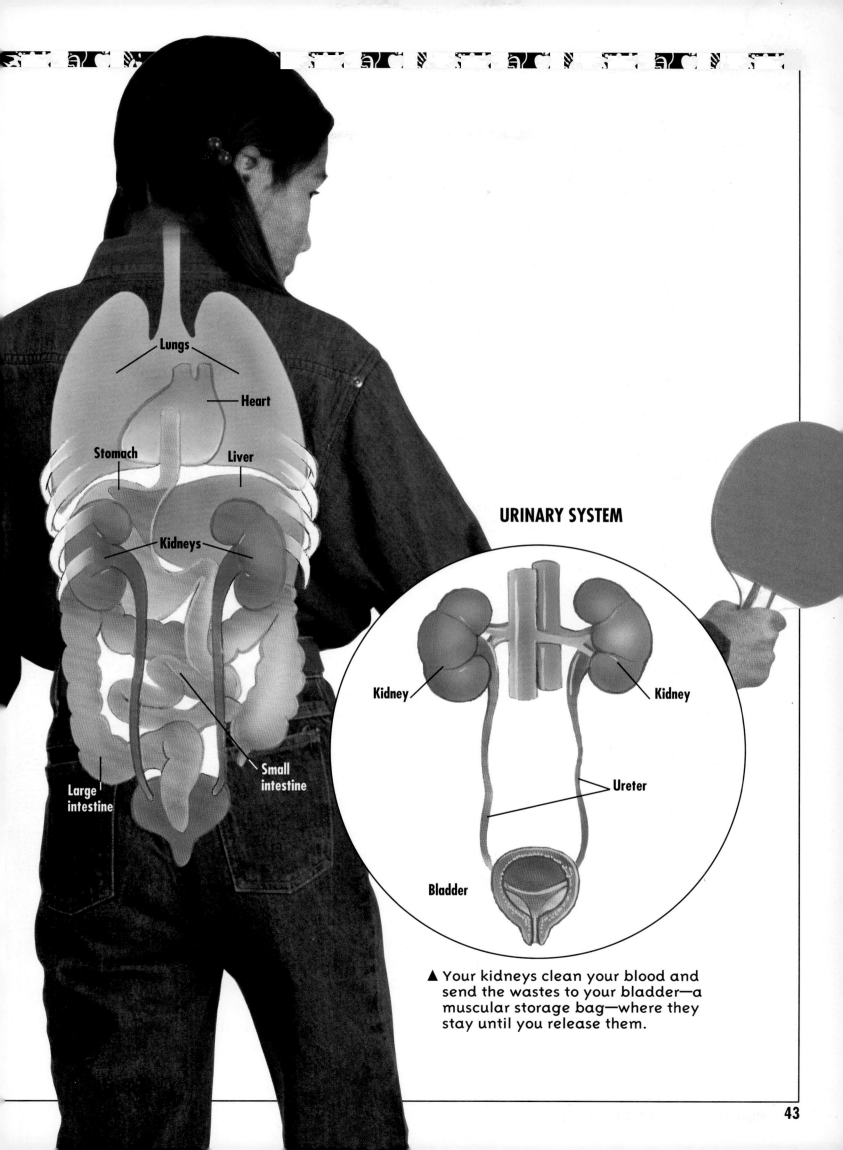

Lungs

Heart

Stomach

Liver

Kidneys

Large intestine

Small intestine

URINARY SYSTEM

Kidney

Kidney

Ureter

Bladder

▲ Your kidneys clean your blood and send the wastes to your bladder—a muscular storage bag—where they stay until you release them.

KIDNEY

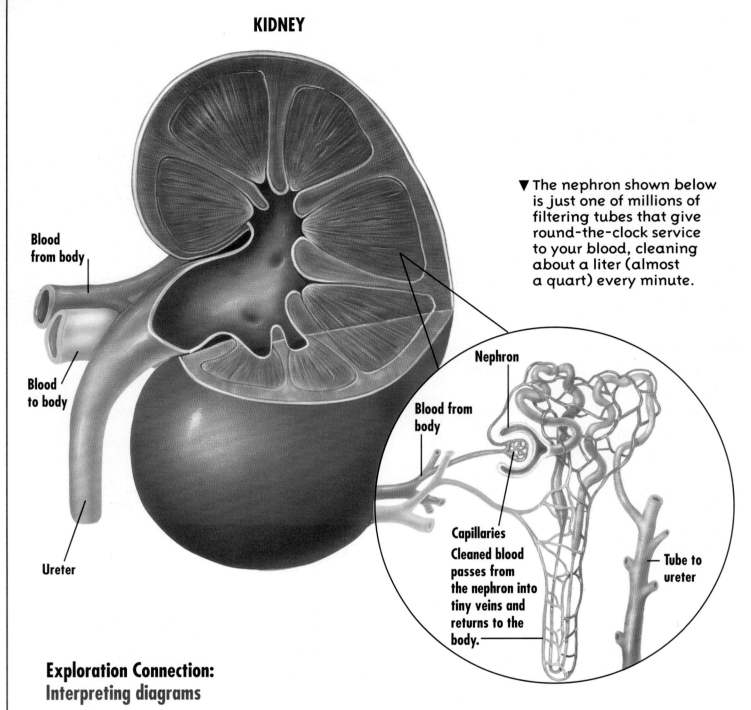

Blood from body

Blood to body

Ureter

▼ The nephron shown below is just one of millions of filtering tubes that give round-the-clock service to your blood, cleaning about a liter (almost a quart) every minute.

Nephron

Blood from body

Capillaries
Cleaned blood passes from the nephron into tiny veins and returns to the body.

Tube to ureter

Exploration Connection:
Interpreting diagrams

When your blood gets dirty, it goes to the cleaners—your <u>kidneys</u>. Your bean-shaped kidneys are wonderful filters that constantly clean your blood. Each of your two kidneys is about as big as your clenched fist. Each kidney contains about a million filtering tubes, like the one shown in the diagram, called nephrons. Blood flows into and out of these tubes, leaving its wastes behind. These watery wastes, called urine, drain into your bladder. Look at the diagram on page 43 and find the tube that carries urine from the kidney to the bladder.

Your blood circulates through your kidneys hundreds of times a day, but you make only 1–2 liters (about 1–2 quarts) of urine a day. Clean liquids in your blood return to your bloodstream.

How does your blood move in and out of your kidneys so easily? Look at the diagram. Find the ball of capillaries. How do you think blood moves through this ball of capillaries—quickly or slowly? Explain. How do you think wastes move from these capillaries into the nephron?

Closer to Home:
Between you and the world

You live inside a kind of glove. It's tough, flexible, and waterproof. It keeps your soft, wet, busy insides safe and warm. It lets certain wastes escape. It controls how much heat leaves your body and how much is kept inside. It's alive! It's your skin.

Skin grows from the inside out. The surface of your skin is made up of dead cells. These dead cells are waterproof. When they dry up and flake off, they're replaced by a new layer of dead cells. Your skin is about 0.02 centimeter (1/12 inch) thick in most places. At your eyelids, it's thinner than a human hair. Where do you think your skin is thicker?

Some of the heat made by your cells is released into the air when you breathe, but most of the heat is released through your skin. (Look at the heat-sensitive photo in Exploration 10 again.)

- In ten years, will you have the same skin you have now? Explain.

▲ Some of the wastes in your blood—such as dissolved salts—collect in glands near the surface of your skin. They leave your body through sweat glands. This one is shown 125 times its real size.

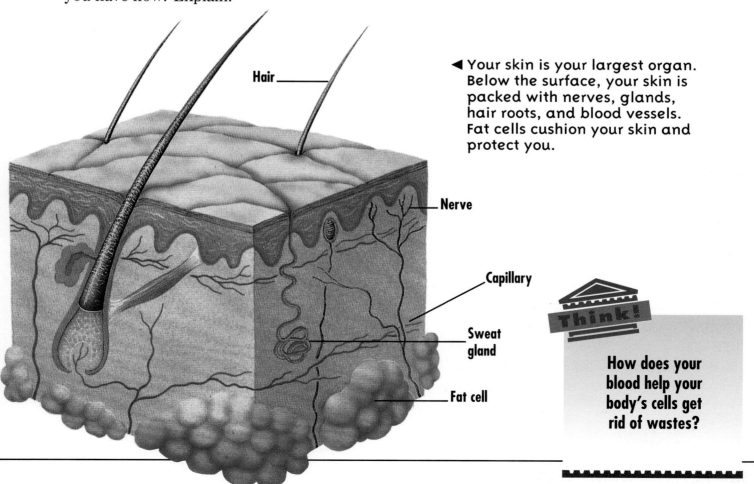

Hair

◄ Your skin is your largest organ. Below the surface, your skin is packed with nerves, glands, hair roots, and blood vessels. Fat cells cushion your skin and protect you.

Nerve

Capillary

Think!

Sweat gland

How does your blood help your body's cells get rid of wastes?

Fat cell

How Does Diet Affect Transport Systems?

Now that you've tracked how your food gets into your cells and out of your body, maybe that old saying makes more sense: "You are what you eat." Foods you eat affect the health of your transport systems. Your digestive system lets you know right away if something disagrees with you. It takes longer to notice the effects of a good diet.

Exploration:
Keep a food diary.

❶ Write down all the foods you eat in a 24-hour period. Don't forget to list what you eat between meals, including gum, candy, soda, and even water.

❷ When your list is complete, sort the foods by taste (sweet, sour, salty, bitter, or combined flavors); by source (mostly plant or mostly animal); by what you like and don't like; and by how often you eat them.

❸ Make a table that shows the way you've sorted the foods you ate.

Interpret your results.

• Did anything on your table surprise you? Explain.

• What, if anything, do you think you should change about your diet?

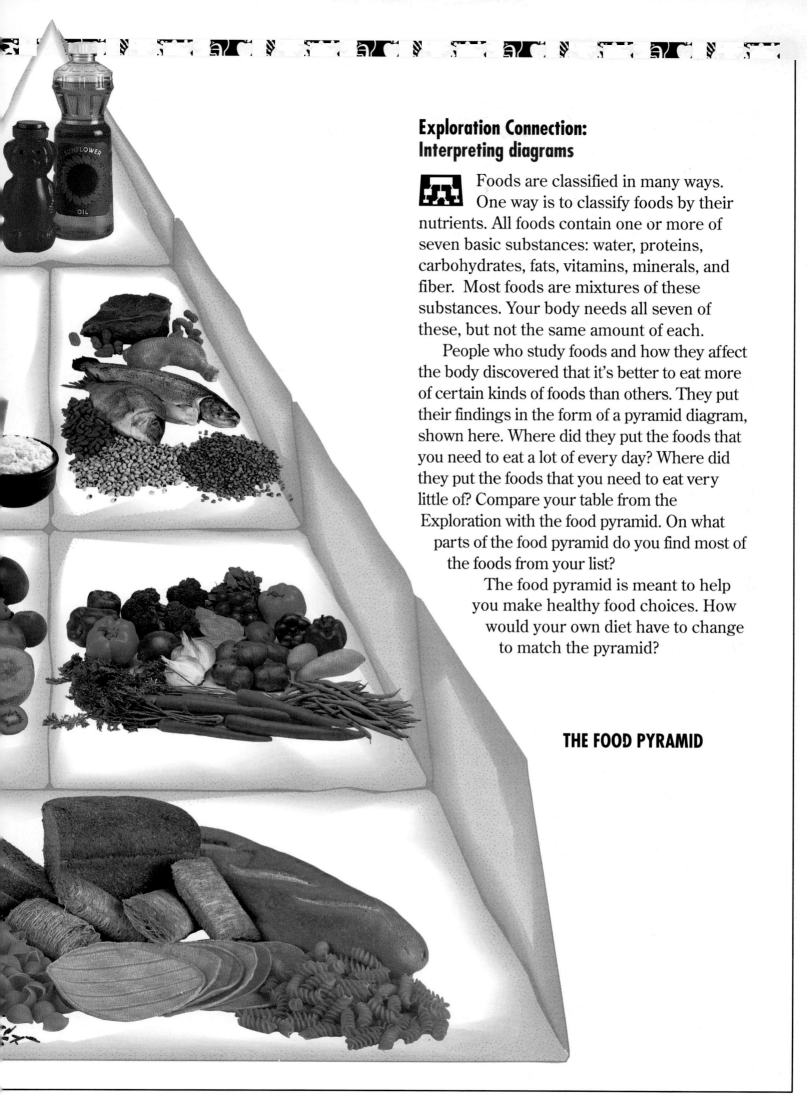

Exploration Connection: Interpreting diagrams

Foods are classified in many ways. One way is to classify foods by their nutrients. All foods contain one or more of seven basic substances: water, proteins, carbohydrates, fats, vitamins, minerals, and fiber. Most foods are mixtures of these substances. Your body needs all seven of these, but not the same amount of each.

People who study foods and how they affect the body discovered that it's better to eat more of certain kinds of foods than others. They put their findings in the form of a pyramid diagram, shown here. Where did they put the foods that you need to eat a lot of every day? Where did they put the foods that you need to eat very little of? Compare your table from the Exploration with the food pyramid. On what parts of the food pyramid do you find most of the foods from your list?

The food pyramid is meant to help you make healthy food choices. How would your own diet have to change to match the pyramid?

THE FOOD PYRAMID

You've recorded what you usually eat during a day. You've compared these foods with the foods you might eat if you followed the food pyramid. Now you have the chance to use what you know to plan your own meals.

Exploration:
Write a balanced eating plan.

You need:
ThinkMat 12
Calendar

❶ Using the chart in your ThinkMat, plan and write a menu for three days. Use the food pyramid as your guide. ✐

❷ List foods you would eat for breakfast, for lunch, and for dinner. Which foods would be good as snacks? ✐

❸ Use the table you made in the Exploration on page 46 to help you include healthful foods that you like.

Interpret your results.

• Is this the first time you've thought so much about food before you ate it? Explain.

• Compare the menu you planned with the foods you actually ate during the past 24 hours. How do your planned meals differ from the meals you've already eaten? Explain.

• What are some reasons for eating a variety of foods?

Serving size ——————

Fat content ◄——————

▶ In the U.S., food manufacturers must put labels like this on all their products. When comparing foods, be sure to check serving size.

CRISPY RAISINS
CEREAL

HIGH IN FIBER

Nutrition Facts
Serving Size 1 Cup (55g/2.0 oz)
Servings per Container 8

Amount Per Serving	Cereal	with 1/2 Cup Skim Milk
Calories	170	210
Fat Calories	10	10
	% Daily Value	
Total Fat	2%	2%
Sat. Fat 0g	0%	0%
Cholesterol 0 mg	0%	0%
Sodium 300mg	13%	15%
Potassium 340mg	10%	16%
Total Carbohydrate 43g	14%	16%
Dietary Fiber 7g	28%	28%
Sugars 17g		
Other Carbohydrate 19g		
Protein 4g		
Vitamin A	15%	20%
Vitamin C	0%	2%
Calcium	25%	15%
Iron	45%	45%
Vitamin D	10%	25%
Thiamin	25%	30%
Riboflavin	25%	35%
Niacin	25%	25%
Vitamin B$_6$	25%	25%
Folate	25%	25%
Vitamin B$_{12}$	25%	35%
Phosphorus	20%	30%
Magnesium	20%	25%
Zinc	25%	25%
Copper	15%	15%

Ingredients: Wheat bran with other parts of wheat, raisins, sugar, glucose, corn syrup, salt, malt flavoring

Closer to Home:
Read before you eat.

Once you start thinking about your own diet, you may want to know more about the foods you like. How can you find out what's really in those highly flavored, brightly colored food things you cheerfully crunch? Check the label. It should look similar to the one shown here. The nutrition label tells you everything that's in the food. Then you can decide if it's good for you.

For instance, you're innocently munching a cracker. Then you notice the label on the box—"sugar, preservatives, additives, artificial color…" You thought you were eating just a plain old cracker! Without the label, you never would have known. Now you can investigate.

- Look at the ingredients of your favorite cereal. Forms of sugar often end in "-ose." Which ingredients do you think are a kind of sugar?

- Some foods don't seem sweet at all, but they contain one or more sugars. What foods do you eat that you don't think are sweet? Check the ingredients. Which ones have sugar in them?

Think!

From what you discovered in your earlier Explorations, which substance do you think your body would miss first? Why?

How Does Exercise Affect Transport Systems?

Eating is probably one of the few things you do that's done best sitting still. Your body is more often in motion, burning up all that food you feed it. One reason you want to eat good foods is to keep your body moving easily and well. Besides using energy, what do you think all that motion does to your body?

Exploration:
Check your breathing rate.

You need:

Clock or watch with second hand
LabMat 9

❶ Look at your clock or watch. Keep count each time you inhale. Record how often you inhaled in one minute.

❷ Compare your resting breathing rate with your resting pulse rate—while you're sitting still. Record how often your heart beats per breath.

❸ Look at your clock or watch and run in place for a full minute. Keep timing and count how often you inhale in one minute. Check your pulse rate again and record your breathing and pulse rates.

❹ Compare your pulse rates to those you recorded in Lesson 9.

Interpret your results.

• How do your breathing and pulse rates change when you exercise?

• How are breathing rate and pulse rate related?

• Can you slow your heart rate by consciously slowing your breathing? **Try it!**

Exploration Connection:
Interpreting graphs

 When you move fast or lift something heavy, your body demands more fuel and needs more oxygen. What can you do to make yourself stronger?

Your heart is a muscle. Exercise that makes your heart pump faster and harder makes your heart stronger. The stronger your heart, the more blood it can pump with each beat. A weaker heart moves less blood per beat, so it has to beat more often.

If you sit around a lot, your pulse rate tends to be higher than if you get a lot of exercise. Look at the graph. It shows the pulse rates of athletes while resting. You know how strong athletes are. They sometimes exercise for more hours a day than you spend in school. Which sports do you think require the strongest circulatory systems?

RESTING PULSE RATES OF FULL-TIME ATHLETES

Athlete	Resting Pulse Rate
	68
	65
Dancer	60
Weightlifter	58
Volleyball player	55
Sprinter	50
Football player	
Oarsman	40
Swimmer	35
Runner (2–6 miles)	

▼ Which of your transport systems do you think are strengthened by running?

Closer to Home:
Move that body!

Unless you're a complete couch potato, you probably get some exercise every day. You might not even think of it as exercise. Do you walk up and down steps? Do you play ball during recess? Do you walk home from school?

People whose jobs require a lot of physical activity—such as carpenters, farmers, firefighters, and dancers—often get plenty of exercise. So do people who spend most of their day standing or walking. People who sit most of the day—like office workers or students—must often pick a special activity they like in order to get the exercise they need. Exercise can be part of a daily routine, just like eating and sleeping are.

- Look at the list below. On this chart, the higher the number, the more the body benefits. What do the activities with a rating over 7 have in common?

- It's a good idea to begin exercising a small amount each day and build up to a big workout. What would happen if you didn't increase the amount of exercise slowly?

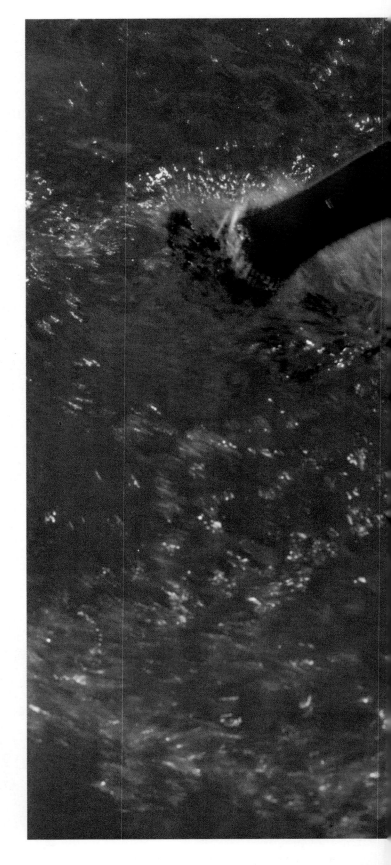

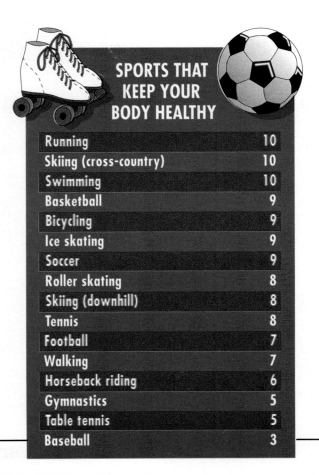

SPORTS THAT KEEP YOUR BODY HEALTHY

Running	10
Skiing (cross-country)	10
Swimming	10
Basketball	9
Bicycling	9
Ice skating	9
Soccer	9
Roller skating	8
Skiing (downhill)	8
Tennis	8
Football	7
Walking	7
Horseback riding	6
Gymnastics	5
Table tennis	5
Baseball	3

▲ In what ways can the activity
shown here affect each of your
transport systems?

Think!

Which kinds of exercise are best for
strengthening your circulatory and
respiratory systems at the same time?

How Else Can You Protect Your Transport Systems?

There are things you inhale that your body doesn't need, and the more you know about them, the less you'll probably want them in your lungs. How do you think damage to your lungs would affect your transport systems?

Some of the things you inhale you can't control easily. Bacteria that cause illness are tiny, light, and easy to inhale. You can't see carbon monoxide, a deadly gas produced by all motor vehicles that run on gasoline. You can see smog, smoke and dust, but you can't always avoid breathing them in. There are some things you can avoid—inhaling tobacco smoke, for example.

Tobacco has dangerous ingredients. One is nicotine, an oily, sticky poison that makes the heart work harder. When tobacco burns, it also produces a tar that clogs and weakens bronchial tubes. Then the body has to work harder to take in the oxygen it needs. Smoking also causes blood vessels to tighten. The heart must pump even harder and faster to move oxygen and nutrients through the blood vessels.

Chemicals in tobacco can also cause cells to change in ways that cause cancer. Most people who get lung cancer are smokers.

Most people know that smoking is bad for their health—the dangers of smoking are printed on every cigarette package. So why do you think people start smoking? If your friends started smoking, how could you defend a decision to not smoke?

▶ Tiny particles containing harmful chemicals fly with the winds. Usually you can't see these things, but your body will react to them if they enter your transport systems.

▲ Tobacco leaves are made into cigarettes. Warnings have been on cigarette packages since 1970.

Information Connection: Using reference books

Controlling what you inhale is one way to prevent damage to your transport systems. What you choose to swallow can also hurt those systems.

Drinking alcohol can be dangerous to your health. Even though alcohol is made from fruits and grains, it has very little nutritional value. Alcohol has lots of calories, but they only help make a person fatter, not healthier. People who drink a lot of alcohol all the time often lose their desire for food. Heavy drinking can damage the stomach, the liver, and the brain.

Alcohol gets into the bloodstream very quickly. It doesn't need to be broken down, but is absorbed into the bloodstream starting at the mouth.

Even small amounts of alcohol can affect the way a person moves and thinks. It can slow down the muscles and brain. How could that be dangerous?

One of the many important jobs of your liver is to protect your body from harmful substances. Your liver collects and breaks down these poisons so they can't damage your body. But as you can see from the picture, alcohol can damage the liver. How could a diseased liver harm your body?

Eating healthful food, exercising, and avoiding substances that can damage your body will help keep your blood flowing freely.

To find out more about how your choices can affect your circulatory system, look on page 37 of *The Heart and Blood*.

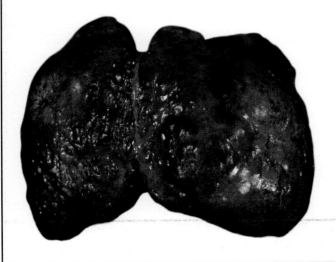

Which is the healthy liver in these two pictures? The diseased liver was damaged by too much alcohol.

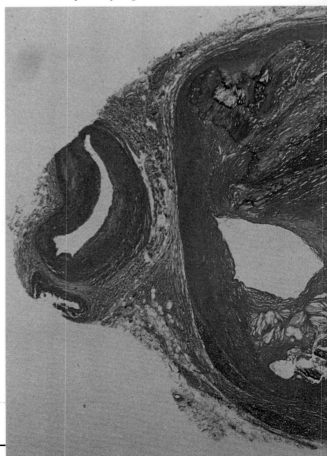

▼ Arteries can get clogged, like this one has, if too much fatty material from fatty foods builds up on the walls of the blood vessels. Compare this picture to the one of a healthy artery on page 33.

Closer to Home:
Clearing the air

Cigarette smoking not only harms a smoker's health, it's also a major source of indoor air pollution. People have strong opinions about the rights of smokers and the wrongs of smoking. Some people say that when they smoke they hurt only themselves. Others say you don't have to smoke a cigarette to inhale the smoke if it's swirling all around you. Scientific research shows that second-hand smoke is very dangerous to your health.

Over 2.7 million children in the United States suffer from <u>asthma</u>, a disease of the respiratory system. This disease is on the rise. Many doctors blame this rise on air pollution—particularly smoke in the air.

Air pollution is bad for everyone, but it does the most damage to people with breathing problems, such as asthma. Cigarette smoke can cause asthma attacks in people with asthma. During such an attack, the muscles around the lungs' air passages tighten. The air passages also get clogged with mucus, which makes it even harder to breathe.

- Many towns and cities are passing laws to keep people from smoking in places where other people would have to breathe the smoke. What do you think about a law like that?

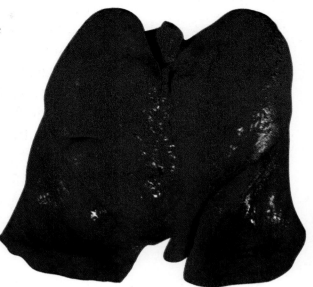

Which are healthy lungs and which are lungs destroyed by cigarette smoke?

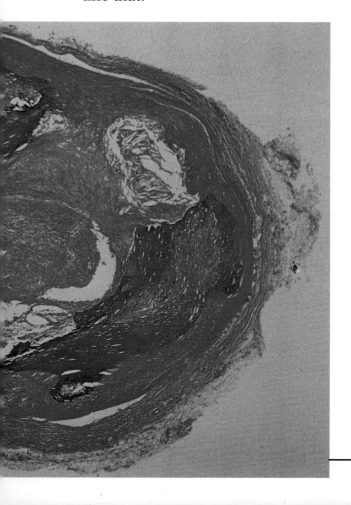

Why do you think there are laws against selling tobacco and alcohol to children?

Identify Problems: Design a Transport Game

Think Tank Road Map

Many people think that the body's digestive, circulatory, and respiratory systems are separate from each other. You know how they're connected and how they help each other work. Imagine that you have to help a younger child learn how they work.

15 • In Lesson 15 you'll identify the problems you'll have to solve to design a board game that shows how the human body's transport systems are connected.

16 • In Lesson 16 you'll identify some possible solutions to those problems.

17 • In Lesson 17 you'll map out a path of transport through the body. Then you'll use the map to make a model of your game.

You may also want to review the video to see how the Science Sleuths went about exploring the body's transport systems.

Problem: A toy company is planning to market an educational board game based on the transport systems of the human body. The company has asked you and your team to design the game. To play the game, players must move their markers through the body's digestive, circulatory, and respiratory systems. The rules are up to you!

These questions will help you make a list of the problems you'll face while trying to design a game based on the body's transport systems:

1 What have you already learned about human transport systems that you'd want to include in a game?

2 How do liquids, solids, and gases move through your body's circulatory, digestive, and respiratory systems? How can you use this information to map out paths of transport for your game?

3 As you design your game, think of what the transport systems do and why the body needs them. What kinds of things does the body's transport system move around? What is the goal of the game? What problems will players solve?

4 The pictures on these pages show different methods doctors use to explore and repair the body's circulatory, digestive, and respiratory systems. You may want to use one of these methods as the big idea in your game.

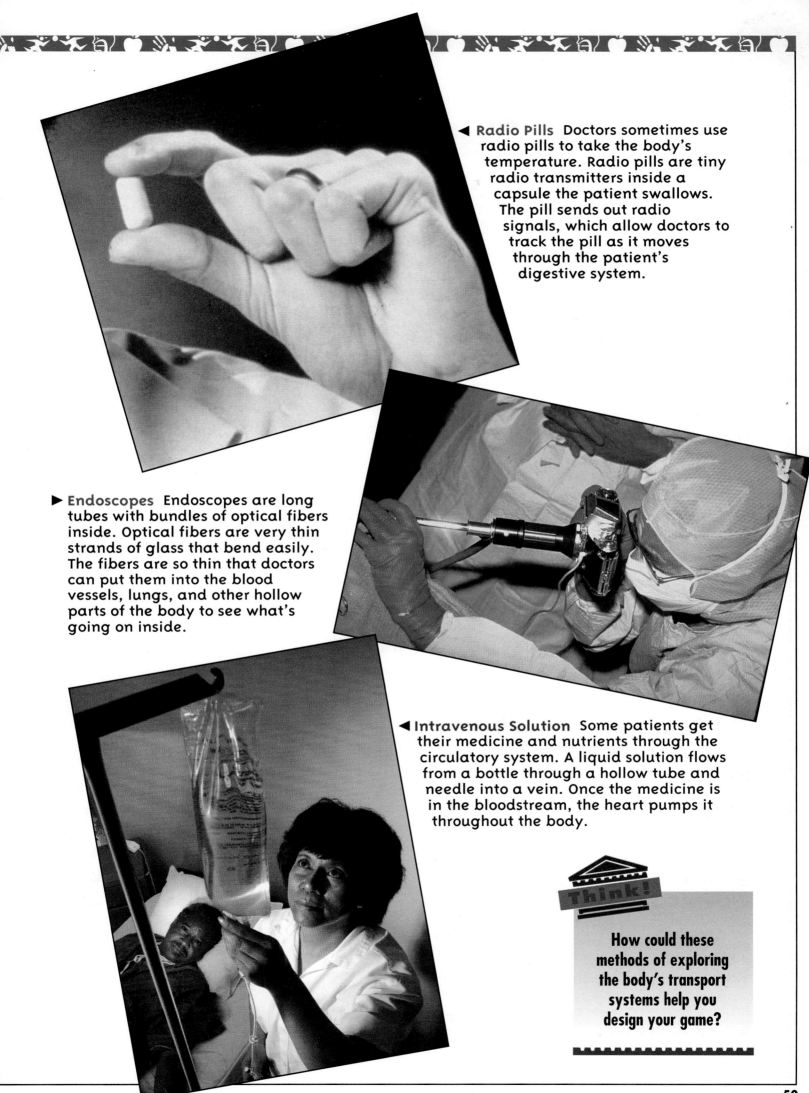

◀ **Radio Pills** Doctors sometimes use radio pills to take the body's temperature. Radio pills are tiny radio transmitters inside a capsule the patient swallows. The pill sends out radio signals, which allow doctors to track the pill as it moves through the patient's digestive system.

▶ **Endoscopes** Endoscopes are long tubes with bundles of optical fibers inside. Optical fibers are very thin strands of glass that bend easily. The fibers are so thin that doctors can put them into the blood vessels, lungs, and other hollow parts of the body to see what's going on inside.

◀ **Intravenous Solution** Some patients get their medicine and nutrients through the circulatory system. A liquid solution flows from a bottle through a hollow tube and needle into a vein. Once the medicine is in the bloodstream, the heart pumps it throughout the body.

Think!

How could these methods of exploring the body's transport systems help you design your game?

Find Solutions: Design a Transport Game

How are white blood cells like a human highway patrol?

White blood cells are the body's rescue squad. They travel through the body's transport systems and help keep the body healthy.

Some white blood cells patrol the lungs and trap dust. Some gather near cuts or scrapes where they can catch germs that get into the body. Some destroy viruses and fight diseases. Some help remove cell wastes.

To do their jobs, white blood cells have to be able to reach every part of the body. They travel with the blood through the blood vessels. When they get to the places they are needed, they leave the transport system through tiny capillaries.

There are millions of capillaries in the body. If they were all put in a straight line, the line would stretch about 96,000 kilometers (60,000 miles)—more than twice around the world.

You've just identified some ways doctors make use of the body's transport systems. Now you'll take a closer look at some of the instruments that allow doctors to "see" inside the human body. Studying how doctors explore the body's transport systems might help you and your team design your board game.

1

Make a chart of the problems you listed in the last lesson. Beside each problem, try to list a similar problem facing the engineers and doctors who design and use these medical instruments.

2

Study the photos and captions. What path through the body does a gastroscope take? a bronchoscope? a cardiac catheter?

3

What are some of the problems that can occur in each transport system? How could these problems affect the ability of blood, air, or nutrients to move freely throughout the system? How can you use this information in designing your game?

4

Brainstorm with your team to come up with possible solutions to each of the problems on your list. Write them down in your chart.

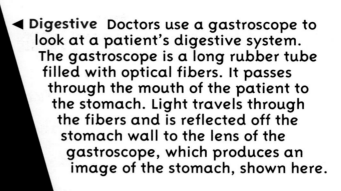

◄ **Digestive** Doctors use a gastroscope to look at a patient's digestive system. The gastroscope is a long rubber tube filled with optical fibers. It passes through the mouth of the patient to the stomach. Light travels through the fibers and is reflected off the stomach wall to the lens of the gastroscope, which produces an image of the stomach, shown here.

► **Respiratory** A bronchoscope is a hollow tube with a system of lights and mirrors that allows doctors to see inside the respiratory system. The bronchoscope is inserted into the patient's mouth or nose and goes down through the trachea, shown here, and into the lungs.

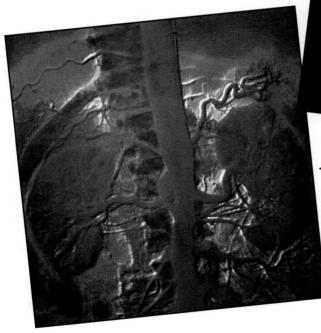

◄ **Arteriograph** An arteriograph is a special kind of X-ray that allows doctors to check the blood supply to any area of a patient's body. Doctors have injected the arteries in this patient's kidneys with a chemical. The chemical allows doctors to see computer-generated images of the arteries and blood vessels on a video screen.

Other resources you can check:

• To find out about a journey through the body: *The Magic School Bus™ Inside the Human Body*, by Joanna Cole. Scholastic Inc., 1988.

• To find out about the circulatory system: *A New True Book: Your Heart and Blood*, by Leslie Jean LeMaster. Childrens Press, 1984.

Think!

How does learning how doctors explore the body's transport systems help you plan your game?

Make Models: Design a Transport Game

Possible models for your transport game:

Diagram Use the diagrams in this unit to help you draw pictures of the transport systems for your board game. Be sure to label the diagram to show how the players' markers will move through the transport systems.

3-Dimensional Model Use cardboard, colored markers, or any combination of materials to actually build your board game. Include all the pieces and instructions necessary to play the game.

Written Description Write a sales brochure that describes every detail of your game— its parts, how it makes use of the transport systems, its instructions, and so on.

Computer Graphics Use a graphics program to design your game on the computer.

Oral Presentation Give a speech about the game as though your team were making a presentation to the toy company that hired you.

Your team has identified problems you'll face in designing a board game based on the body's transport systems. You've also identified possible solutions to some of those problems. Now you'll use those solutions to make a model of your game.

1

Will your game include all three transport systems? If so, will you show all the systems in one diagram of the body, or will you use a separate diagram for each system?

2

How will a player win? Will the players move their markers around the board by throwing number cubes? by correctly answering questions about the transport systems?

3

Work with your team to design the game. Make a model based on your design. Choose one of the models shown on this page.

4

Look at all the models your class has made. How did different teams solve problems? Play another team's game. Does playing help give you new ideas for the game?

5

After you revise your game based on the ideas other people give, test the game with a group of younger children.

6

What were the most important things you learned in this unit that helped you design your game?

Resources for designing your transport game:

• Your journals or LabMats from this unit are filled with valuable data you've collected and conclusions you've made about human transport systems.

• Look back at the graphics and information in Lessons 1–14 of this Student's Map.

• The reference books you've used in this unit are filled with lots of additional information.

• Refer to the Video Clue Log. What characteristics of the human transport system did the Science Sleuths investigate?

• Talking to another team may help you solve a difficult problem.

Think!

How did making a model of your game help you think of problems and solutions you didn't think of before?

FOR SCIENCE BROWSERS

Why Do I Get Hiccups?
from *National Geographic World*

© Danielle Jones 1994

How embarrassing. You're at the library; all is quiet and then . . . *hic!* Oh no. You've got the hiccups. Everyone gets them, and everyone has a suggestion for curing them—drinking water, eating sugar, scaring them away. Breathing deeply or holding your breath may stop them, but they usually go away by themselves. No one knows what causes hiccups, but we do know what happens. The diaphragm, a powerful muscle that helps you breathe, suddenly contracts, pulling air into the lungs through the voice box. The air slams shut a flap on the voice box that keeps food out of the wind pipe. When air hits the closed flap, the nearby vocal cords go *hic*.
—*June 1993*

Itty-Bitty Machines

by Hank Hogan
excerpt from *Boys' Life*

Imagine a robot so small it could swim through your blood vessels. A doctor would inject it into your bloodstream where it could unclog an artery or battle an infection.

That sounds impossible today. So did space travel less than 60 years ago. But tiny machines that perform big miracles may be just over the horizon. Scientists already have built gears, motors, levers and tweezers that you can see only through a microscope.

The itty-bitty motors spin. The microscopic "tweezers" pinch closed when voltage is applied. The day may come when these flea-sized machines can do much more in the fields of medicine, manufacturing and protecting the environment.

"Micromachines" are so small you could fit several of them inside this "o." They are half a millimeter across, about the width of six human hairs. Some are even smaller. One motor is only about two-thirds the width of a hair.

These tiny machines are useful because many things are just too small for regular-sized tools to handle. You can't cut a human cell with a knife, for example, or grab a bacterium with tweezers.

Today, doctors regularly send tubes through people's blood vessels to look inside their bodies. With micromachines, it may be possible to put tiny scissors at the end of such a tube. That way, a doctor who needed to test cells for disease could collect them without operating. Tiny tools would cause less damage to the body than surgery and be less stressful for the patient.

Some scientists dream of a day when major surgery may not be needed to battle heart disease. Instead of a surgeon operating, tiny robots could be sent through the arteries to scrub away the fatty deposits that cause heart attacks.

How Micromachines Are Made

Most micromachines are made from silicon, the same material used to make computer chips. Silicon is an element found in very pure sand.

To build the toothed wheels of a tiny turbine, technicians first stack layers of silicon. Using a special camera, they print the image of a gear on the stacked layers. Then they use chemicals to etch away everything that isn't covered by the wheel image. What's left is the toothed wheel.

Using silicon allows scientists to build the tiny machines *and* their controlling electronics on the same chip. That keeps the size of the tools small. Thousands of the machines can be made at the same time, so each one costs very little.

—*May 1992*

"Excuse my borborygmus!" That's what you might say the next time your tummy growls. The noise with the weird name is caused by gas moving inside your stomach or small intestine.

He Takes Hip-Hop to Heart

by Francelia Sevin
excerpt from *Science World*

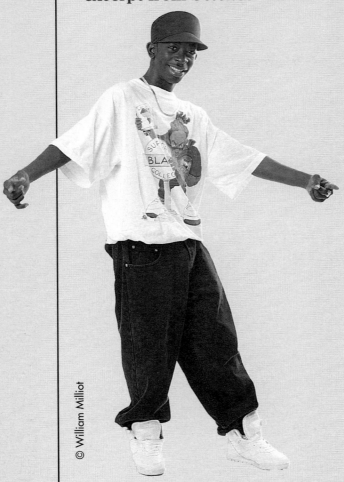

© William Milliot

Sixteen-year-old Tasheen Carrow, a.k.a. Scram, is physically fit, flexible, and funky. His secret: Dance hard, dance often.

When Tasheen Carrow hits the dance floor, people take notice. His moves are electric, and he never slows down. As long as he's on the floor, it's high-octane hip-hop. No wonder rap acts are paying Tasheen— known as Scram in the hip-hop world—top dollar to appear in their videos.

Packed with so many strenuous moves, his routines push his body to the limit. So Scram—like all serious athletes—stays fit by working out nearly every day. But you won't catch him riding an exercise bike or lifting weights. "I get all the exercise I need from dancing," he says.

Heart-Starting Moves

No arguments there. Hip-hop dancing is great for *cardiovascular fitness.* That is, it strengthens your *heart.*

With every pump, the heart sends oxygen and nutrients to all the muscles in the body. The muscles use these materials as fuel to do work. And the stronger the heart is, the more efficiently it can deliver this fuel. So by keeping his heart fit, Scram makes sure he has the energy to stay on the dance floor long after his rivals have worn out and gone home.

But hip-hop dancing is more than an affair of the heart. All that jumping, bending, and stretching helps to make the muscles in Scram's body strong and flexible. *Strength* and *flexibility* are essential to physical fitness. They enable Scram to pull off tough moves like hitting the splits and bouncing back up to the time of the beat.

Thumping's Up

You too can dance your way into great shape. A twenty-minute work-out (that's four or five songs) three times a week can do wonders for your heart, lungs, and the rest of your body.

But remember, slow waltzing won't cut it. To make dancing an *aerobic workout*—the kind that improves your cardiovascular fitness—you've got to get your heart thumping. How fast? Here's an easy way to find out: First subtract your age from 220. Then multiply by .70. What number did you get? That's how fast your *heart rate*—the number of beats per minute—should be to give your heart a good workout. Are you dancing hard enough? Take your pulse and see.

Before you hit the floor, though, Scram advises that you take a few minutes to stretch out and warm up. "It makes you more flexible so you can dance better," he says. A warm-up will also help prevent muscle pulls.

In no time, you'll be moving, and feeling, great. —*February 1993*

How Does Laughing Help Your Health?

by William Fry
from *SuperScience Blue*

Laughter can give you a workout! In fact, 100 good "belly laughs" are as good for your body as 10 minutes of boat rowing. Why? Try this:

Laugh hard! (You may need help from a funny friend, your favorite comic strip, or a TV comedy show.) While you laugh, feel the muscles in your stomach, chest, neck, and shoulders. Which tense up?

One other muscle works hard when you laugh: your heart. It beats faster.

All that good exercise can help keep you healthy. But what if you're already sick? Researchers have found that laughter:

•**Helps you heal.** Scientists have found that laughter makes your white blood cells more active. These cells are like tiny bodyguards that fight disease and infection.

•**Makes patients happy.** And happy patients seem to get well sooner, say some doctors. At the very least, the patients complain less and need less medicine. One hospital keeps patients "in stitches" by lending out funny books and tapes.

Did you know that even a *fake* smile or laugh can make you feel good? Try this: Look in a mirror. Slowly say "oh-oh-oh" about 10 times. How do you feel? (Besides silly . . .) Then say "ee-ee-ee" about 10 times. Do you feel any different? Which sound made you look most like you were smiling?

•**Cuts down on harmful stress.** Could laughing flood your brain with naturally relaxing chemicals? Some scientists think so. The chemicals are called *endorphins* (en-DOR-fins). They cut tension, ease pain, and help you rest. —*April 1992*

Don't Forget to Brush
The only human tissue that doesn't change naturally between childhood and old age is part of the digestive system. That tissue is tooth enamel, the hard covering of your teeth. Take good care of it!

© Michael Krasowitz/FPG

Warning: Smoking Harms Non-Smokers, Too

by A.T. McPhee
excerpt from *Current Science*

You smell *it*. Cigarette smoke. A couple of kids are puffing on cigarettes just a few feet away. You cough. Your eyes tear. You feel queasy.

Recent studies suggest frequent exposure to someone else's smoke greatly increases a nonsmoker's risk of developing cancer or heart disease.

As many as 32,000 Americans who don't smoke may die each year from heart disease brought on by passive smoking. The term *passive smoking* refers to a nonsmoking person's breathing either smoke blown into the air by a smoker or smoke that drifts off the end of a lighted cigar or cigarette. Researchers at the Veterans Administration (VA) Medical Center in Kansas City, Mo., found recently that passive smoking causes tiny blood cells called platelets to clump together. This clumping, say the researchers, could lead to a heart attack.

Platelets are tiny cells that stop blood from escaping a broken blood vessel. Normally, when a blood vessel breaks, platelets flowing through the bloodstream form on the damaged vessel. A chemical in the blood makes the platelets suddenly sticky. The stickiness causes the platelets to clump together and stick to the lining of the injured vessel.

A clump of platelets, together with other substances in the blood, forms a blood clot. The clot seals the broken vessel and stops the bleeding. Clots can also form in blood vessels that aren't broken, blocking the normal flow of blood.

Such blockage may prove deadly. If a clot blocks the flow of blood through a heart artery, for instance, the heart may not receive enough oxygen-rich blood to survive. The result: a heart attack. Thousands of smokers die each year from heart attacks caused by blockages of major blood vessels in the heart.

Experts now say nonsmokers run a similar risk of blockage. According to the VA researchers, platelets in a nonsmoker begin clumping together within a mere 20 minutes of breathing someone else's smoke. Years of repeated exposure to a smoker's smoke, say experts, can prompt continued buildup of platelets until the vessel clogs and a dangerous heart attack strikes.

Smoking doesn't cause just heart attacks. It can also cause cancer. Doctors say chemicals in tobacco smoke can damage cells, sparking abnormal growth of the cells and the eventual development of cancer.

Now doctors know exactly where some of these changes take place. Dr. Erika Randerath, a researcher at Baylor College of Medicine in Houston, Tex., recently discovered a number of specific changes that occur in heart cells, lung cells, and other cells in smokers.

The way to avoid getting cancer from smoking, of course, is not to smoke to begin with.

Forever Young
Some organs of your digestive system shed the cells that form their lining about once every three days.

A recent study of school systems across the U.S. found that 95 percent restrict smoking in some way. Researchers say a growing number of high schools and middle schools restrict smoking not just for students, but for teachers as well.

For the sake of your health and the health of others, won't you just say no, too? —*September 1990*

Sneezing Season

by Marilyn Greenwald
excerpt from *Boys' Life*

Thirty-five million Americans suffer from allergies. Something as small as a grain of pollen or dust can trigger sniffling, sneezing and watery eyes.

Some people are unlucky enough to have food allergies. Yummy things like ice cream or chocolate can cause them to sneeze or get red, itchy bumps called hives. Such symptoms are their bodies' ways of fighting foreign invaders.

A Family Affair

Allergies are not contagious, so you won't catch them from other people. You're more likely to inherit them from your parents. If they have allergies, you may have them too. The good news: Some allergies that are severe in childhood lessen as you grow older.

As uncomfortable as they are, few allergic reactions are dangerous. You can avoid the symptoms by avoiding the substances that cause the reactions, called "allergens."

Common allergens include:
- things you breathe: dust, animal fur dander, grasses, weeds, molds;
- things you eat: nuts, eggs, milk and chocolate;
- things you touch: poison ivy and poison oak.

Check Out Your Home

If you have allergy symptoms all year long, you are probably allergic to something inside your home. It might be something as simple as dust or animal fur. Clean your home two or three times a week.

Some allergies pop up only part of the year. Pollen or spores probably are the culprits. These seasonal allergies often are called hay fever.

Food and drug allergies can be tough to detect. If you suspect you are allergic to a certain food, keep a diary of everything you eat for a week. Soon, you will be able to link the reaction with the food.

If you have an allergy but cannot pin it down, see a doctor. Tests can reveal the cause of your misery. A small change in the way you live might be all you need for relief. —*September 1993*

You Can Live Without It

Do you know anybody who's had his or her appendix removed? The appendix is a small worm-shaped tube found close to the place where the small and large intestines join. If food gets caught in it, the appendix can become infected. Removing the appendix seems to be the best way to solve that problem, and losing the appendix doesn't seem to have any effect on a person.

So long!

GLOSSARY

Concept vocabulary and other technical terms

arteries [är'•tər•ēz]: *n.* Thick, muscular vessels that carry blood away from the heart to the rest of the body.

asthma [az'•mə]: *n.* An illness in which the air passages in the lungs are narrowed or clogged and breathing is difficult.

bronchial tubes [brong'•kē•əl t(y)o͞obz]: *n.* The two main branches of the trachea, or windpipe, that lead to the lungs, or any of the tubes branching from them.

capillaries [kap'•ə•ler•ēz]: *n.* The narrow, threadlike blood vessels that connect the arteries with the veins.

circulatory system [sûr'•kyə•lə•tôr•ē sis'•tem]: *n.* The parts of the body through which the blood moves.

diaphragm [dī'•ə•fram]: *n.* A strong sheet of muscle that separates the lungs from the organs below it.

digestion [dī•jes'•chən]: *n.* The process of breaking down food into nutrients— tiny particles that can pass through cell walls into the bloodstream.

digestive system [dī•jes'•tiv sis'•təm]: *n.* The system of parts of the body that digest food.

esophagus [i•sof'•ə•gəs]: *n.* The tube that food passes through as it moves from the mouth to the stomach.

gastric juice [gas'•trik jo͞os]: *n.* A thin, watery fluid produced by the stomach to aid digestion.

kidneys [kid'•nēz]: *n.* The organs that separate excess water and waste products from the blood and release them as urine.

large intestine [lärj in•tes'•tin]: *n.* The short, thick, lower part of the intestine.

mucus [myo͞o'•kəs]: *n.* A thick, slimy substance produced by glands in the body.

oxygen [ak'•si•jən]: *n.* A colorless, odorless, tasteless gas that makes up about one fifth of Earth's atmosphere.

plasma [plaz'•mə]: *n.* The fluid part of blood.

platelets [plāt'•lits]: *n.* Tiny circular or oval bodies present in blood and necessary for clotting.

red blood cells [red blud selz]: *n.* The cells that carry oxygen in the bloodstream.

respiratory system [res'•pər•ə•tôr•ē sis'•təm]: *n.* The parts of the body through which oxygen enters and carbon dioxide is removed.

small intestine [smôl in•tes'•tin]: *n.* The longer, narrower portion of the intestine, leading from the stomach to the large intestine, where nutrients are absorbed into the bloodstream.

veins [vānz]: *n.* Muscular, tubelike vessels that carry blood back to the heart from every part of the body.

white blood cells [wīt blud selz]: *n.* Cells that attack and destroy germs in the body.

a	add, map	ī	ice, write	û(r)	burn, term
ā	ace, rate	o	odd, hot	yo͞o	fuse, few
â(r)	care, air	ō	open, so	ə	a in above
ä	palm, father	ô	order, jaw		e in sicken
e	end, pet	o͝o	took, full		i in possible
ē	equal, tree	o͞o	pool, food		o in melon
i	it, give	u	up, done		u in circus

Page references in *italics* indicate illustrations, photographs, and tables.